Babynomics

Madeline Thomas

This edition first published in Great Britain 2010 by
Crimson Publishing, a division of Crimson Business Ltd
Westminster House
Kew Road
Richmond
Surrey
TW9 2ND

A catalogue record for this book is available from the British Library.

ISBN 978 1 90541 065 1

Printed and bound by LegoPrint SpA, Trento

Contents

Acknowledgements

No book is complete without some requisite thanks to those who have helped shape the book or shared their knowledge.

Thank you to Crimson Publishing – to Beth for finding me and helping get the idea off the ground and to Sally for her huge organisational skills, attention to detail and a brain that functioned far better than mine. Thanks to BabyKind, Babyworld, The Children's Mutual, Citizens Advice, Daycare Trust, Halifax, Liverpool Victoria, Mumsnet, NannyTax, National Childbirth Trust (NCT), Nationwide, and Netmums, for allowing me to quote them or their surveys.

A huge thank you to Which? for letting me use their invaluable resources (you will see just how helpful they are when you read the book) and to Money Saving Expert Martin Lewis for being similarly generous with his time and his resources.

A big thank you to mums and dads, both up and down the country and overseas, who happily shared their parenting thoughts and tips simply because all mums love a bit of good money-saving advice. So, thank you to everyone who emailed, phoned, Facebooked, texted, poked or even just stopped me in the playground for a chat. You know who you are (as we all do now you're in print!!). Thank you. You were invaluable.

Last but not least, thank you to Arthur and Eve for giving me so much material to use in this book and for being truly inspirational; and to Geraint for helping me, supporting me and believing it would all be worthwhile. Let's hope he's right!

Maddy

The big number

The average cost of raising a child from birth to adulthood is a staggering £201,000.

When I first read that number I thought there must be some mistake. After all, you could buy a house for that. (OK, a small-ish house, but a house nonetheless.)

There is no mistake.

Now my children are growing up fast, I've realised just how much they cost me. The result of this realisation is twofold.

Firstly, I'm hugely appreciative of the efforts my parents made and the sacrifices they had to make to raise me and my sister. They survived a three-day week, inflation of 24%, unemployment of more than three million and still managed to make ends meet.

Secondly, I've realised that no matter how prosperous we become as a nation, each generation faces similar financial struggles when it becomes their turn to raise children. We are a wealthier country than when my parents were raising me. Back then people ate home grown vegetables and made their own clothes out of financial necessity rather than a lifestyle choice. However, it is wrong to judge today's parents by the standards of the 1970s and 1980s. Children's clothes were a lot more expensive. Food was seasonal or expensive. People didn't eat out. If they did venture to a restaurant once a year it was for a prawn cocktail or soup followed by steak and chips and Black Forest gateaux, washed down with a lovely bottle of Mateus Rosé that could be used forever after as a candlestick.

Today, food is cheap so the focus has shifted to sourcing nutritious food at a good price. Many clothes are cheap too, especially now that supermarkets have expanded their range to include clothing.

Today's parents face other financial strains. The cost of accommodation takes up a significantly larger portion of household income than it did two decades ago. Higher education has gone from costing many families little or nothing (due to the grant system and lack of tuition fees), to an estimated £23,500 (the Push student debt survey) for living costs and tuition fees over a three-year degree.

Looking at the work the friendly society Liverpool Victoria does in tracking the changing cost of raising a child over the years, it is apparent that this cost is rising faster than the rate of inflation – in other words, we are spending a bigger chunk of our earnings each year to do the same job.

It is hardly surprising that education and childcare costs have soared. What is interesting is how families have coped. Pocket money is lower now than it was two years ago and we're spending less on holidays now than we did five years ago.

Breaking it down

So, here are the eye-watering stats: we spend nearly £55,000 on childcare, £53,000 on education and £11,000 on babysitting in the 18 years it takes to raise a child. OK, so second and subsequent siblings might get a 10% reduction on nursery fees but that still means shelling out the best part of £50,000 for each of them. Then there are the wider living costs to take into account. That means adding £17,000 for food, £14,000 for clothes and £13,000 for holidays. It's easy to see how this money soon adds up to the more than £200,000 each child costs to raise.

This book is not designed to change how you raise your children. It has merely been written in response to these astronomical costs.

It lays out the significant financial decisions and the practicalities that parents face at various stages of their child's development: pregnancy, birth and the first year, the toddler years, pre-school, primary school, the teenage years, and managing university without sinking under an unmanageable debt burden.

The book is intended to be used as a guide too. Hopefully, it will help you to address:

- What the costs are at each stage.
- Which costs are avoidable.
- Which costs are not avoidable.
- Which costs can be trimmed.
- What difference that will make to your lifestyle decisions.
- When and how you need to take those big parenting decisions.

Learning the hard way

When my son was born, I was the first one in my group of friends to have children. I was also the first one in my family to have children, as was my husband. There were no cousins, neighbours or anyone we knew who had kids from whom we could borrow kit. As I was working for a dotcom company at the time, the workforce was young, so I was also the first of my colleagues to have kids. It meant we bought everything from scratch and it cost us a fortune. I simply did not know where else to go for good quality, affordable baby kit. In fact, I didn't even know there was an alternative at that stage.

I wasn't alone. Plenty of other mothers I met at antenatal classes were in a similar position.

Yet this longing for a bit of inside knowledge of how to go about each stage in your child's (and your family) development continues. It is probably hardly surprising therefore that I hear the following phrase so often:

'I WISH I KNEW THEN WHAT I KNOW NOW'

Hindsight is a wonderful thing. This book is full of it. It is full of the experiences and words of wisdom from parents who have found methods to suit them. It is also full of practical common sense.

Child rearing is phenomenally expensive and that expense kicks in with a fantastic sense of irony – it occurs just at the time when many parents curtail their career ambitions (or their earning power) and creates a financially painful double whammy.

Because of that, this book looks at some wider aspects of finance – after all, sorting your complete money picture is often the only way you will be able to afford to make the lifestyle and child rearing decisions that are right for you.

I'M STILL LEARNING

As a financial journalist and a mother of two, much of the content of this book has been shaped by my parental experiences and my knowledge of the financial difficulties parents face. However, as part of the process of compiling the experiences of other parents and drawing on the knowledge of experts, I have changed how I go about certain issues.

Take, for example, pocket money. I will be awarding pocket money very differently from now on. I will also be taking a less controlling approach in how my children spend their money so they can make their mistakes while they're still young enough that it doesn't matter, but old enough that they can learn from those mistakes and become more financially aware.

I've shuddered at the cost of hobbies, childcare, education and financing a degree and I will be encouraging greater and earlier saving from my two so they can help bridge the finance gap for themselves.

I also never thought I'd get my kids to go through the household finances in their teenage years but, having looked at how we acquire financial knowledge and just how money savvy extremely young adults need to be, I will now make it part of their annual household chores!

A little note about prices

All prices shown throughout the book:

- □ Were correct at the time I researched the book and may not be correct at the time of going to print.
- □ Have been rounded to the nearest pound.

Please also note that as different retailers have different offers on, depending on the season and manufacturers' end of lines etc, the examples used are, by their nature, time sensitive.

1. Pregnancy

what you should and
shouldn't buy

Early lessons

Whether or not your pregnancy has been long awaited or a bit of a surprise,
Mother Nature has thankfully ensured you have nine precious months to
prepare for the baby's arrival.

You'll need it.

You are likely to receive a great deal of advice and information. Much of
it will conflict, and much of it is entirely unnecessary. This book is not a
pregnancy and birth manual so thankfully it will sidestep a lot of issues your
friends and family, health visitor, antenatal classes, new parent magazines
and neighbours might cover.

However, it *will* look at the purchases impending parenthood might compel
you to make and help you to not waste money. It will also look at how
having a baby might change your life, or influence your approach to the
work/life balance, and look at how you can best afford to make the life
choices you wish to make for the benefit of the whole family.

Whether this pregnancy fills you with unbridled excitement or blind terror there is no escaping the fact that it will hurl you headfirst through an entire gamut of emotions: joy, pain, love, panic, and even hysteria. But parenthood will not only drain your emotions (as well as bring unbridled joy), it will also drain you of every available financial resource, and more, if you let it.

> ❝ Jack gets hand-me-downs from a friend. When he's finished with them we pass them back and his mum passes them on to someone else. Likewise, we pass all of Daisy's clothes on to my goddaughters and in return they've given us a pushchair and toddler bed for Jack. ❞
>
> Katy, mother of Daisy and Jack

Most family and friends, magazine articles and baby books will talk about the need to prepare for your imminent arrival by researching, testing and buying baby kit.

Yes, there's a lot to do, but not nearly as much as the baby industry would have you believe.

There's certainly lots to buy. But that can be a problem in itself. There are **too many** things expectant parents can buy and a whole industry geared up to encourage them to do just that, sometimes unnecessarily. Bath thermometers might tell you the precise temperature of your bath, but an elbow does the job just as well – our parents managed with their elbows so I'm sure we can too. As for baby baths themselves, some parents find them really useful. However, many other parents I know found out a little too late that their baby bath didn't sit properly on top of their existing bath so they couldn't use it AND they had nowhere to store the thing. And no-one, but no-one needs a baby wipe warmer.

In short, this chapter is about which new purchases for babies are genuinely worthwhile and which are best avoided.

After all, the cost of raising a child is as much as a mortgage (£201,000 from birth to 21), so there's little point in being over-eager to buy everything new from the off. That way madness (or a stonking great overdraft) lies.

BABIES COST £1,560 BEFORE THEY'RE EVEN BORN

Research conducted back in 2006 by baby milk manufacturer SMA Nutrition showed parents spent, on average, £1,560 on their babies before they were even born.

- A third of that amount was spent on maternity wear, health supplements and magazines.
- One in seven parents spent between £2,000 and £2,500.
- Prams and pushchairs were the single most expensive item, costing most people more than £200.
- Baby carriers and bottle warmers were considered the biggest waste of money.

So, you see, it is far too easy to spend hundreds, if not thousands, of pounds on trying to do the right thing for your child.

TOP TIP: BE RUTHLESS, DON'T GET CARRIED AWAY

When they look back, many seasoned parents are appalled by what they bought in the early days (and how much it cost) when it became clear that a lot of the kit was simply not needed.

Maternity wear

It's not all about the baby. Mum needs to look – and feel – good too. Luckily, these days there are some great maternity clothes that needn't cost the earth.

One of the best places to buy new maternity clothes is H&M. Their clothes wear well, wash well and are good value. Mothercare also does good essentials. However, don't go mad. There's little point in buying more maternity outfits than you need for a first pregnancy on the proviso that you intend to have more children because sometimes things simply don't work out that way.

> *"My first child was born in a hot, sticky mid August at the end of an extended hot summer. I lived in linen trousers, flip flops and smart, loose shirts for work. My second child was born at the end of January. In fact, it snowed the night she was born.*

I invested in two maternity skirts (one corduroy, one denim)
a decent cardigan and a couple of long-sleeved maternity
tops. All these winter items were hard wearing and went on to
clothe three of my friends afterwards."

Maddy

The essential clothing list

- ◻ Two items of comfy maternity legwear (jeans/trousers or skirts)
- ◻ Two or three stretchy tops
- ◻ One cardi
- ◻ One smart outfit that you can customise for important work meetings and going out

When smock tops are in fashion, expectant mums don't have to worry about maternity tops – their existing tops accommodate their growing bump. If fashions change, don't despair. Wear one of your partner's shirts for hanging round the house at the weekend and purloin his tracksuit trousers (assuming he's bigger than you!). That way, the only items you have to finance are ones for going out and about.

TOP TIP: MAKE SURE YOUR MATERNITY JEANS FIT

Buying maternity jeans that fit is as difficult as buying regular jeans that fit properly. Don't buy them thinking they will fit better when your bump gets bigger. If they fit badly round the tops of the thighs and across your bottom when you buy them, they'll still fit badly when your bump gets bigger. Instead you could...

- Extend the life of your normal jeans for as long as possible by looping elastic between the button and button hole and wear extra long tops over them.
- Tie a scarf around your stomach as a bandeau to hold everything in place (kooky but stylish).
- Bump bands – £10 new or from secondhand NCT and Netmums sales – do the same job.

HIGH STREET VS DESIGNER

Marks & Spencer, H&M, Top Shop and Mothercare are great high street places to shop for basics. For those who prefer shopping from home,

Littlewoods and Next catalogues also have a wide range of good value staples.

However, having a wardrobe full of basics is great but sometimes they just don't hold up to scrutiny. I had a wedding to go to when I was 36 weeks pregnant with my first child and I was on TV on a weekly basis so I had to look good. That is when something a little different might be called for.

Designer maternity wear is available from:

- Jojo Maman Bébé
- Blooming Marvellous
- Séraphine
- Mamas and Papas
- ASOS.com (more usually associated with recreated red carpet glamour at a fraction of the price)

IF YOU WANT SNAPPY MATERNITY DRESSING ON A BUDGET, GO SECONDHAND

Netmums' nearly-new sales can be good places to find maternity wear. Their discussion boards are also good places to ask for help in finding secondhand maternity gear. For dates of your local nearly-new sales, go to www.netmums. com. The other great place is Freecycle (www.freecycle.org). By signing up to your local Freecycle newsletter in good time you are almost certain to find someone wanting to get rid of perfectly good maternity clothes in your size.

IF YOU ARE BUYING RATHER THAN RECEIVING FOR FREE, CHECK:

- Seams
- Waist fastenings (especially check that the elastic is still good)
- Whether the fabric has bobbled
- How many pregnancies the item has been worn for
- How it washes

You should be able to find a maternity outfit that would cost £100 new for under £20.

Buying new for your newborn

Expectant parents – especially first time parents – have lots of time to prepare for the arrival of their infant making it all too easy to invest too much time, effort and money on the first few weeks and months of a baby's life. By that, I mean investing in seemingly 'must-have' nursery accessories such as a new Moses basket and stand, a room thermometer, an expensive baby bath and oodles of designer attire.

Newborn babies are masters of projectile expulsions – from both ends – and everything baby wears or sleeps in could end up covered in milk, puke, wee and poo several times a day. So, why not shun the designer kit (that's what indulgent grandparents or single friends are for!).

Luckily, there are still items that should be bought new for your baby, so there is plenty to mull over and get excited about. There are also plenty of bargains to be had online and in charity shops, not to mention favourite items that friends, family or neighbours may be only too keen to pass on.

TOP TIP: DON'T BE A SNOB

Shop around, choose carefully and don't be too proud to ask (or even beg) for baby kit. By shopping around and getting as much as you can for nothing you should be able to kit out house and baby for a lot less than £1,560. Don't be a snob. Hand-me-downs should be a baby's staple.

See the table at the end of this chapter for a rundown of how I kitted out baby for less than £250 when researching this book.

And don't forget, this is the exciting bit. The newsagent's shelves are literally bulging under the weight of baby magazines all testing different products and all extolling the virtues of the latest in baby innovations. Of course, these all cost money – it is only right that parents should buy some of them new but, quite frankly, the rest can be begged, borrowed or bought secondhand.

To my mind, there are only four things that really have to be bought brand new:

- □ The baby car seat
- □ The cot and/or cot bed mattress

☐ Baby monitor/sleep alarm sensor

☐ Baby milk bottles

CAR SEAT

Buying a car seat is a matter of safety. Even if a car seat looks fine you have no idea whether it has been in a car that has crashed and therefore whether it has suffered hidden damage. Some car seats come as part of an integral pram, which in turn costs hundreds of pounds. I have addressed prams and travel systems separately in this chapter, because there are more issues to consider when looking at them. If you are considering a travel system (which includes a car seat), then please read the section on prams too. For now, let's just focus on car seats.

Mothercare or Halfords are both great places for trying before you buy. By that I mean they have display models which you can often try in your car (under supervision, of course). Both have a wide variety of makes and models in stock and a free fitting service, to ensure you and your partner know how to attach the seat safely. Both also offer discounts online that they don't necessarily pass on in-store. So, before you part with your cash, do some research.

1. Go online and look at the makes, models and prices on offer through websites such as Kelkoo, Amazon.co.uk Baby, Mothercare, Halfords, Babies 'R' Us, Argos and Kiddicare.com. Look at own-brand makes and compare them to coveted names such as Britax, Mamas and Papas or Maxi-Cosi.

2. Check whether any of the seats you are looking at have won any awards, such as a 'Mother and Baby Award' or a 'Which? Best Buy'. It is a useful stamp of approval but not the be-all and end-all of car seat buying.

3. Think about what type of car seat you want. There are two broad types:

    ☐ Infant car seats – rear-facing only for children up to 9kg (20lb) in weight (up to age nine to 12mths)

    ☐ Combination seats – rear facing until the child reaches 9kg (20lb), and then forward facing until 18kg (40lb) in weight (age three to four years)

4. Can you ISOFIX? There are many different ways car seats can be secured in your car. ISOFIX systems are considered the most secure, and the easiest to remove your child from in the event of an emergency. ISOFIX seats have a plastic base that is secured using two or three ISOFIX securing points within your car's rear seats. The baby's car seat simply clicks into place on top. All cars built since 2002 should have ISOFIX points in place, but they sometimes come as an option (albeit at no cost) rather than as standard. So, check what type of seat your car can take before you buy. If in doubt, get advice from the likes of Mothercare or Halfords (see above).

5. Choose the right seat for you and the family, not just the child. This might depend upon whether you are planning more children; how closely together in age you plan to have them; and whether it could be more economical to have a seat for each stage for the children to share. Alternatively, you might prefer to deal with any subsequent children as and when they turn up. Each family is different but do consider your options.

6. Take your research with you to a shop and ask the experts any questions you may have.

7. Check your car's rear seatbelts are long enough to stretch around the infant seat of your choice. I remember walking to my mother's house from the train station carrying my child on one visit while she drove home with my bags in the car. Her rear seatbelt wouldn't stretch around my son's seat and therefore it could not be secured. Suffice to say, always check before you buy.

8. Subscribe to the online voucher code service **www.vouchercodes. co.uk**. It often has 10% off vouchers from Mothercare, which you can either print off and use in-store or online. Don't worry if you don't have your own computer or printer at home: you can still find the deals on their website and all libraries now have decent computer and printer facilities.

9. Research done, go to your nearest computer armed with all your information and **buy online**.

TOP DEAL

Here's just one example I found using the Britax First Class Plus combination car seat:

- Online and in stores most offered this seat (in selected fabric finishes) for an RRP of £140.
- Argos sold it for £120.
- Halfords had it for £100.
- Mothercare online, Kiddicare.com and Babies 'R' Us all offered the seat for £90.
- However, Mothercare also had free delivery and if you could take advantage of a timely voucher code, you'd get a further 10% off the price, taking it down to just £81. Bargain.

Total savings: £59

However, Mothercare's own combination seats cost just £45 and Kiddicare.com's just £60, so it is possible to drive down the cost even further.

COT MATTRESS

There is absolutely nothing wrong with buying a Moses basket, cot or cot bed secondhand, provided it meets current safety standards (see pages 23–24). In fact, it's an ideal arrangement. However, health professionals would advise you to buy a new mattress.

Research into Sudden Infant Death Syndrome (SIDS/cot death) suggests that children sleeping on secondhand mattresses are at greater risk of cot death. Of course many families with more than one child don't rush out and buy a new mattress for each of their subsequent offspring to use (and neither did I), yet the evidence suggests that even children from the same family are at greater risk of cot death by sleeping on a hand-me-down mattress.

So, a new mattress is a must and worth the cost.

Make sure you choose a correctly sized mattress, so choose the cot or cot bed first. If in doubt, make sure your secondhand cot comes with a mattress and measure it carefully in order to buy a true like-for-like replacement.

A cot or cot bed mattress can cost anything from £30 to £175, depending on what type you choose. The main three types are foam, coil sprung and pocket sprung.

The obvious places to shop are retailers such as Mothercare and Kiddicare. com. However, thanks to online retailers and discount warehouses, there are ways of buying a new mattress for about half of their prices. Websites such as Kelkoo and eBay are good places to shop. However, do check customer feedback on the e-tailers you are thinking of buying from before you part with any cash. Feedback should tell you how reliable the retailer is and the level of service you can expect. Also, don't forget to factor postage costs into your overall shopping bill.

 TOP DEAL

I shopped for a 120cm x 60cm cot mattress.

- Foam Core mattress from Mothercare = £33 (free delivery)
- Foam Core mattress via eBay e-tailer was £20 + £6 p&tp = £26

Total savings: £7

- Coil sprung mattresses from Mothercare cost between £65 and £90
- East Coast Coil Sprung mattress from Amazon.co.uk was
  £37.50 + £2.50 p&tp = £40
- New Coil Sprung cot mattress + extra cover from eBay was
  £30 + £13 p&tp = £43

Total savings: £25–£50

BABY MONITOR

Some seasoned parents will disagree with my wisdom here but there is method in my madness.

Not all parents subscribe to baby monitors. However, those who do tend to swear by them and use them for years. Ours came in particularly handy on summer evenings when we wanted to sit in the garden, when visiting friends or relatives where the house layout was different, and on holiday. Other parents I know, with older, boisterous children, kept their listening monitors in the kitchen while their infants were having daytime naps so they could hear if anything was wrong above the din of the toddler siblings.

To use or not to use such devices is entirely your choice.

CHECK FORUMS AND WEBSITE FEEDBACK SECTIONS BEFORE YOU BUY

- Kiddicare.com has reviews posted by parents and these can be really useful in helping you decide which product is right for you. You get a sense of how people use the item you're considering purchasing and whether they have encountered any niggles or issues that would also be a bugbear for you.

- Netmums is also good place to search for feedback. Alternatively, you can ask a question on their forum and wait and see what answers you get back. Really useful.

- Mothercare online has an advice section on big ticket items that includes issues you may want to consider before you buy.

In fact researching and buying all the big ticket items at the same time might save even more money as some sites offer free delivery when you spend over a certain amount.

For those who are unlucky enough to know of a cot death in the family, there are listening devices available that monitor signs of movement during your child's sleep through a sensitive pressure pad that is placed under the cot mattress. If the pad doesn't sense any movement for 30 seconds or more, an alarm sounds. While such devices will not stop heartbreaking tragedies from occurring altogether. They may – in families with a particular concern – help parents to sleep more easily at night knowing there is an extra layer of watchfulness over their baby. Find out more about reducing the risk of cot death at **www.dh.gov.uk**.

For those who are hearing impaired or who prefer a visual clue, some monitors now come with integrated cameras so you can see as well as hear your little one.

But why buy one? Because parents who opt for monitoring devices tend to love them so dearly, they also tend to be very well worn and well travelled. During their lifetime wires can come loose and they may not monitor as effectively as they did when new. So, if you are going to buy one, buy new and buy a recommended model. It will last for second and subsequent children and will be money well spent.

As with car seats, it is worth going around a specialist baby shop and looking at the make and model you want before searching online for the best deal. It may seem like a lot of legwork but you want to make sure you're not wasting your money.

 TOP DEAL

I searched for a new baby monitor under £50.
- Tomy Walkabout Classic Advance (via Kelkoo) costs £38.50
- Tomy Walkabout Classic Advance (via Mothercare online) was £32

Total savings: £6.50
- BT Digital monitor (via Mothercare) was £50
- BT Digital baby monitor (via Kelkoo) costs £40

Total savings: £10
(Author's note: Kelkoo is just a search engine that trawls websites to find the cheapest deals. It won't cover all websites, so use it in conjunction with other methods.)

❝❝ What a lot of parents seem to do here as a way of reducing costs is join a website called Freecycle. Often it has baby and kids stuff and that seems to go quickly. I guess it saves trawling around charity shops. For those giving stuff away I guess it saves them trying to auction items on eBay or taking it elsewhere as takers come and collect goods. It is a great idea and a way of recycling goods, hence the name! ❞❞

Caroline, Australia, mum to Ben

BABY FEEDING BOTTLES

> ## BOTTLE FEEDING FACT
>
> Each year, around 720,000 babies are born in the UK. By the time they're six weeks old, more than three quarters of them are completely bottle fed. Many more babies have at least one feed a day from a bottle.
>
> *(Source: Babyworld)*

Health facts and stats

Chemicals called plasticisers are used in the manufacture of plastic bottles. Bottles containing polyvinyl chloride (PVC) contain plasticisers called phthalates. Bottles manufactured using polycarbonate plastics contain plasticisers called bisphenol-A (known as BPA, for short).

Both phthalates and BPA are known as hormone disrupting chemicals and they may, in some instances, be a contributory factor to certain adverse health effects ranging from infertility to premature puberty, asthma, allergies and even breast and prostate cancers. BPA is used in thousands of plastics everyday, not just baby bottles. However, as infants could be particularly susceptible to BPA, how baby bottles react is crucial.

BPA can be released from baby's bottles which have been subjected to bottle brushing, dishwashing or sterilisation. So in short, while baby bottles are generally safe, parents can take basic steps to make sure they stay safe:

- Discard worn bottles (those that are cloudy or scratched): chemicals leach into food more easily when plastics break down.
- Do not fill bottles with boiling water.
- Don't leave plastic baby bottles in hot cars or direct sunlight.

This means avoiding secondhand bottles as these will generally be scratched.

Some baby bottles are now BPA-free. They include makes such as:

- Medela
- BornFree
- Lansinoh
- MAM

If in doubt, check the bottom of the bottle. It should say what's in it.

For babies needing around six feeds a day, it make sense to stock up on six bottles with matching newborn teats.

Steam sterilisers can be bought new or secondhand. After all, they're sterile! Alternatively, sterilising fluids such as Milton are still available from Mothercare and Boots.

(£) TOP DEAL

- Pack of three BPA-free Medela bottles costs £8
- Six newborn teats cost around £10
- Kiddicare.com had an offer on Tommee Tippee decorated bottles (BPA-free) at just 99p each!
- They also had a Close to Nature cold water steriliser for £10 (reduced from £22.47).
- Bibs and/or muslin squares **will** be an essential part of a newborn feeding kit. Mothercare sells a pack of five bibs for £5. Supermarkets also sell bibs cheaply. Mothercare sells a packet of 50 top-and-tail muslin squares for £7.

Total set up cost: £35–£40

Buying secondhand

This is where the fun really starts. In order to start successfully buying secondhand, you need to know which outlets sell what items (or give them away). New parents are better prepared than ever before, thanks to the internet and its marvellous ability to convey information.

The thing is, there's nothing like a bit of experience to tell you what you can buy secondhand, where to get it from, and how much you should spend. For that reason, to help shape this chapter (and indeed this book), I have spoken to mums and dads up and down the country about their experiences, their financial regrets, their good buys and bad buys and what they might do differently if they had had the hindsight then that they have now.

So, peppered throughout this book are phrases and tips from mums and dads that will hopefully enable you to avoid making the same costly mistakes.

❝ I was a lot more 'wise' about what I needed for my second baby, and regretted a lot of wasted money from my first (like the very expensive off-road buggy that took up our entire hallway and was frowned upon in many a crowded cafe or shop) so a good tip would be to talk to mums of older babies about what they found useful, rather than being influenced by what the first time mums-to-be in the antenatal group are buying. ❞

Belinda, mum to Harry and Adam

Scary it may be but babies become **more** expensive as they get older, not less, so avoid buying anything new unless you absolutely have to. There will be plenty of time and opportunity to throw money at your child(ren) in years to come.

Before you go secondhand crazy, there is one piece of advice to remember: don't buy anything you cannot clean thoroughly. Most people have looked after their items really well and would be mortified at the thought of them being considered dirty. However, if you, for example, purchase an item from a house with pets and your child has allergies, it could cause all sorts of problems. This shouldn't stop you taking the secondhand route; it simply means thinking before you buy.

TOP TIP: IF YOU CAN'T WASH IT, DON'T BUY IT

- Only buy fabric items (toys/clothes etc) secondhand if they can be machine washed.
- Clean all secondhand items thoroughly, including hard plastic ones, before letting your infant use/play with them.

This rule may sound alarmist but it is just common sense. Many hospitals and playgroups these days have a policy of only accepting plastic toys that can be cleaned with disinfectant to limit the spread of germs. Of course a few germs may be a healthy way to build up a child's immune system but there is still no sense in taking unnecessary risks. So, if you can't wash it, don't buy it.

PRAM/TRAVEL SYSTEM

There are so many different prams, buggies, strollers, travel systems, twin buggies, and toddler options, that the choice can be overwhelming. Most parents I have come across (myself included) have ended up with at least two different models: a proper pram for when the baby is small and a buggy for toddlers.

Ok, now's the time to introduce some jargon busting so you know what I mean.

- **Travel system**. A super-duper pram with car seat clip on/off option. Some are wheeled bases that then have varied clip options for a lie-down pram, standard 5-point harness sit/recline pushchair and removable car seat/carry cot option. Others don't need the lie-down cot because their strollers recline fully.
- **Pram**. Most prams have two functions. A carry cot for very young babies and then a standard sit/recline pushchair
- **Buggy**. Basically a lightweight easy-to-fold pushchair suitable for infants six to nine months onwards. Strollers are versatile, easy to take anywhere and become more essential as infants get older.

Good buggies come in at about £100. Sometimes you can find fantastic buggies secondhand that still have a lot of life left in them. However, buggies are probably one of the most used pieces of infant kit so they can get pretty battered. This is the sort of item that needs a thorough look at before you buy secondhand. Check for wear and tear and, if in doubt, don't buy.

As for prams, they can cost more than £500 when new. One I saw cost an eye-watering £850. What's more, like cars, there are lots of 'optional extras' that bump up the price, some of which really are essential (such as rain covers).

So, what are the options for secondhand prams?

eBay

Pros:

□ There is a wide variety of secondhand prams and travel systems available, many of which have been hardly used and some of which are brand new.

□ The savings can be enormous and many will come with cosy toes, matching nappy bags and rain covers, saving around £50 on optional extras.

□ Sellers are encouraged to list all flaws on their items to improve their feedback rating, so if you have an honest seller you'll know what you're really getting.

Cons:

□ Although many are in good condition, some really aren't and photos can be taken from the best angles, meaning you won't always see the flaws before you buy.

□ Do you know, for example, that the pram system you're buying collapses properly or that all the elements attach on to the wheel base properly?

□ There is a danger that the excitement of the auction may cause you to overspend. So, either stick to 'Buy It Now' items and only pay a fixed price or give yourself a maximum price, bid in the last 30 seconds of an auction and be decisive.

(£) TOP DEAL

- I'coo pram that was clearly brand new with detachable carry cot, pushchair, car seat, matching changing bag and raincover for £50, for collection in Cornwall (around £200 new).

- Mamas & Papas pram, carry cot & pushchair system offered in Essex area for £20 (around £500 new).

- Quinny three-wheeler pram, for collection in Lancashire: included carry cot, changing bag and raincover. Only damage was a tear in the rear pocket. It sold for £24 (approx £650 new).

- Silver Cross Linear pram/pushchair for £100 (around £395 when new).

Total savings: between £150 and £625

NCT nearly-new sales

NCT is the National Childbirth Trust. The charitable organisation is most famous for its antenatal classes but it also has some great nearly-new sales. Each area runs its own sales, where parents can sell their good quality equipment and Philippa, who organises three nearly-new sales a year for one of the NCT regions, says there are normally some great bargains to be had.

The NCT can be contacted at **www.nct.org.uk**.

> Every sale we get about 10 buggies. Sometimes we get mostly double buggies and then other times they are all singles. At the moment we are not seeing the popular brands/fashion brands such as Bugaboo very often but there is always a Mamas & Papas or Maclaren or something like that.
>
> Philippa, NCT sale coordinator

Pros:

- Things sell for a lot less than in the shops.
- There is plenty of opportunity to try before you buy.

Cons:

- There is no guarantee you'll find what you're looking for.
- NCT sales can be a bit frenetic. If you go to an NCT sale, go prepared.
- Turn up with cash, sensible shoes, sharp elbows and quite possibly someone to shield you from pushing and shoving if you're shopping while pregnant.

 TOP DEAL

NCT – nearly-new sale
Bugaboo Frog pushchair £150
Retail price: £379–£419

Total savings: approx £229–£269

Netmums nearly-new sales

Netmums – the nationwide online forum for mums – also organises nearly-new sales on a regional basis. In fact, much of its community based advice and information is done region by region. The sales are of a similar quality and items fetch a similar price. It might simply be a question of finding which nearly-new sale is nearest to you and offers the most convenient options to explore.

CRIB/MOSES BASKET

Many parents prefer to put their infant down for a sleep in a Moses basket or crib in the first three months or so because they're so small and like to feel secure and snuggled. However, it seems ludicrous to buy one new when your child will barely spend any time in it before outgrowing it. Luckily, NCT sales tend to have Moses baskets aplenty, as do charity shops.

 TOP DEAL

- New stand: £20–£30
- New basket: £30–£65
  = Total new cost £50–£95
- Moses basket and stand from NCT nearly-new sale or from charity shop costs about £10.

Total savings: £40–£85

Freecycle
Baskets and stands are often listed on Freecycle. The point of Freecycle is that it is free, so they would cost nothing if you found one.

Total savings: £50–£95

COTS AND COT BEDS

Health facts and stats

Before considering purchasing a secondhand cot, bear in mind current safety advice. Older cots often have poorly designed bars and slats, which can either trap a child's head or fingers, or become dislodged and dangerous. It is now recommended you either buy a new, modern cot or make sure that the slats are no more than 6cm ($2^3/_8$ inches) apart on an older model. Corner posts should not be higher than $1^1/_2$ mm ($^1/_{16}$ inch) above any side railings as items worn by a child or placed in the cot can become caught around them. Cots should also not have any cut-outs in the head and foot panels where small fingers and toes might become trapped, and if the cot has a drop-down side panel, make sure all parts are in excellent working condition with no give in any direction. The general rule is the older the cot, the higher the risk, so most modern secondhand cots should be fine.

The risk to your child in having something secondhand lies predominantly in the mattress, so if there is money to be saved, it is in buying a cot or cot bed secondhand. Again, eBay and NCT sales are good places to start shopping. Alternatively, ask friends and family if anyone they know has children who are outgrowing their cot. After all, cots are bulky items and while many people will go to the effort of selling their unwanted kit on eBay, others don't.

Other places to look for bulky children's items are on church and community centre notice boards (where playgroups are often held) and in primary school newsletters.

 TOP DEAL

The typical cost of a new cot is £100 and a cot bed is £150, although prices range from £60 to £500.

- eBay secondhand cots and cot beds sell for between £15 and £60 plus £10 p&tp
- NCT nearly-new cots are selling for around £15–£50
- Charity shop cots cost around £30
- School newsletter cots are often for as little as £5, plus buyer collects.

Total savings: £85 for a cot and £100 for a cot bed

OTHER BARGAINS

So far, this chapter has taken a piecemeal approach to the big ticket items new parents need. There are plenty more bargains to be had, and plenty of places from which to source them.

These include

- ◻ High chairs (or booster feeding seats that can be strapped to kitchen chairs).
- ◻ Prices range from £11 to £120 depending on make, model and

whether you're buying new or secondhand. A new Chicco Polly high chair costs £120. You could get it discounted, but still new, from Mothercare for £85. You could also get one new from eBay for £87 or secondhand for between £20 and £25. However, a new strap-on chair booster seat can cost as little as £15 new.

□ Baby slings. The BabyBjorn Active sells new for around £86. Secondhand from Mothercare online and Kiddicare.com costs £75. New on eBay costs £55 (+£6 p&p) and good quality secondhand on eBay costs around £20–£30. NCT sales and charity shops cost from £15.

□ Toys and clothes.

□ Bottle steriliser.

□ Baby baths. These can be picked up for free from friends or neighbours or for next to nothing (from £1) from charity shops.

□ Books.

❝❝ My baby best buy was an all-singing, all-dancing Mamas and Papas high chair for £10 from my local NCT sale (they retail at around £100 new). ❞❞

Catherine, mum to Annabel and Harry

There is a list of essential kit for the first three months of your baby's life and sensible prices to pay for each item at the end of this chapter.

Freecycle

Freecycle is a wonderful invention. Basically, it is a facility where people can ask for specific items or give things away, knowing that the person who collects them has a use for them. Freecycle is popular amongst parents, from Cardiff to Cairns (emails I received from Australia demonstrate it is just as popular over there as here in the UK), especially as children grow.

❝❝ I was recently introduced to Freecycling ... I mentioned I was looking to off-load some baby stuff and someone mentioned lots of parents use the site and all you have to do is say what you want or what you want to offer and arrange a mutually convenient time to pick stuff up. You have to register and are restricted in how many wants you post. I think I now have a possible new home for my old pram! 〝

Jane, mother to Ellen and Edward

Most of the time, Freecyclers tend to offer baby and children's clothes (usually bagged in age bundles), books and toys. Occasionally there are bigger items like pushchairs and I have seen cots advertised too. For those needing more general furniture such as a chest of drawers or wardrobe, they can also sometimes be found. Visit **www.freecycle.org** for more details.

Pros:

- Everything is free – that's the purpose of the site.
- You get to email or phone the donor to ask any questions you like and make sure it's what you want before you turn up.

Cons:

- There are no photos on the site, just a brief description of each item and basic contact details for more information.
- It is possible you could arrange to collect something only to find it is not at all what you expected, or it's in terrible condition. You don't have to take it, but you might feel as though you've wasted your time.
- You are also at the mercy of what other people are choosing to off-load, so you could look every day for a month and still not find what you need.

Car booting

Car boot sales are still popular and with good reason. They are great for picking up general baby kit – and for haggling for a bargain. Clothes, books and toys can easily be found and can be bought for as little as 10p an item. Car boot sales may have gained a reputation for selling any old rubbish but, for baby and toddler kit, that's simply not the case. Parents rapidly acquire far more 'stuff' than they could reasonably need or they find their children have grown out of much loved toys and equipment and they have nowhere to store these things. Many parents I spoke to had found big ticket items at their local car boot for very reasonable rates. They included:

- ◻ Stair gates for £5
- ◻ Baby bouncers and door bouncers (although check the fastenings) for £2
- ◻ High chairs for £5 (retailing at between £30 and £150)
- ◻ Baby slings for £10 (retailing at £70–£100)
- ◻ Steam sterilisers for £2 (retailing at £20–£45)
- ◻ Climbing frames and Wendy houses for the garden from Little Tikes for just £10 (they usually retail for between £80 and £600)

The trick is to get to your local car boot sale early, bring the biggest car that you can beg or borrow for the day and take cash with you.

Pros:

- ◻ You can see the goods and examine them properly before you haggle, so you know exactly what you're getting .
- ◻ The chances are you'll save a fortune.
- ◻ Car boot sales tend to be better value than eBay.

Cons:

- ◻ There is no guarantee you'll find anything close to what you're looking for.
- ◻ You might set the alarm for 6am on a Sunday and haul yourself off to a farmer's field in the middle of nowhere only to be disappointed.

School fetes and school notice boards/newsletters

These are a regular source of information for parents wanting to prepare for their baby's arrival on the cheap. Many schools these days have a website with a classifieds section. There is nothing wrong with contacting your local primary school and asking if they have a newsletter or a buy/sell sheet. After all, you'll be dropping your infant off there each morning before you know it!

TOP TIP: SCOUR SCHOOL NEWSLETTERS FOR BARGAINS

I lose count of the number of cot beds, toddler bikes, feeding chairs and infant car seats I see advertised in the school newsletter. The trouble is, most fellow parents already have school age children so there isn't the demand for these products and they end up going for nothing. Bad news for the sellers; great news for you.

Church halls and community centres

Church halls and community centres will probably become part and parcel of everyday life as you get out and about with your infant. From parent and toddler playgroups to drop in centres and even postnatal fitness classes, these big spaces are a great community resource.

Most have at least one notice board and it's always worth scouring to see what's on offer. Some have dates of nearly-new sales; others allow people to advertise specific items. Most NCT sales happen in places like this, as do jumble sales and other fundraisers. All are ideal places for you to snap up essential kit. So, to grab the best bargain, try being a bit nosey!

Parenting networks

There are three big online forums out there:

- ◻ Netmums: www.netmums.com
- ◻ Mumsnet: www.mumsnet.com
- ◻ Bounty: www.bounty.com

All have chat rooms where parents can compare notes and obtain some valuable advice. Netmums also works on a regional basis and, despite its name, can be used by both mums and dads. It organises nearly-new sales and has great forums where parents can swap notes on anything from childcare, to which items wear the best, to baby-friendly shops.

I saw one forum advertising a stroller for £10, a designer pram for £100 and bags of good quality clothes starting at £5 a bag. All three websites are great, but everyone tends to find one to suit them. Browse each and find what suits you.

Charity shop bargains

Charity shops have become the mainstay of many a high street in recent years and they are a boon for new parents.

If your child starts off in a pram and Moses basket but you are thinking of moving them into a cot and using a buggy, visit your local charity shops and see whether they have any suitable furniture in stock. Sometimes they have items in the back which they simply cannot display because they don't have the room so it's always worth asking if you're looking for something specific.

It's also worth bearing in mind that certain charity shops get more baby items than others (and they tend to be ones that raise money for children). So, the Shooting Star Children's Hospice or Save the Children often have more baby kit available than, say, Mind or Oxfam.

I have seen the following, in mint condition, in charity shops:

- Twin stroller for £10
- Moses basket and stand also for £10
- Infant winter coats costing £1
- Items of clothing from 50p
- Books and toys from 10p to £5, depending on the item
- Baby bouncer for £5
- Cot for £20

TOP TIP: BROWSE CHARITY SHOPS WEEKLY

Browse regularly and make charity shopping part of your weekly routine, perhaps on the way to or from the playground. You'll get a regular look at what's new, the staff will get to know you and they might then contact you if they get suitable big items – like pushchairs – in the store.

Most charity shops have infant and toddler supplies coming out of their ears, from videos (yes, they do still exist!) and DVDs, to toys, books, clothes and furniture.

As your child grows and you start wanting to acquire books and toys, visit your local charity shops first. For a start off, you can see what your little one likes to see/touch/play with so you know your money will be well spent. You will be doing your bit for the planet by recycling rather than buying new AND you get to support a charity into the bargain.

Friends and family

For some friends and family money could well be tight. For others, the arrival of a new baby is the perfect excuse for a little retail therapy. As parents, if someone asks you whether you'd like something specific for your infant, BE HONEST. Think about the likely budget of the buyer and pick something you might not otherwise buy that gives them a chance to choose. Remember that they will want to choose something that will last and that will give pleasure.

Examples of suitable presents	Likely cost
A baby bouncer – ideal for the first year of a baby's life	£20–£60
Play mat	£30–£60
A mobile	£10–£35
Funky night light	Around £25
Baby monitor (see page 15)	From £40
Christening/naming ceremony outfit	From £10
Smart clothes	From £10
Cot bumper/bedding	From £15
One or two big ticket items (such as cot or pram) for grandparents/aunts/uncles to club together and buy	From £100
Little indulgences such as sheepskin cot liners	From £30

This list is not designed to be prescriptive (although some department stores, such as John Lewis, do offer baby list services). Instead, it is the result of talking to many mums about what presents they found useful, what their family and friends wanted to buy and what they were happy to receive.

As parents, your job is to fund the essentials. After all, no-one else wants to buy nappies, wipes or infant milk formula as a gift. Given the choice, I bet they'd much rather buy one of those baby hats with the ears on top (visible and fun), so give them a chance to indulge. It means you can save your energies and resources for life's necessities.

TOP TIP: LET FRIENDS AND FAMILY INDULGE

Give friends and family the opportunity to indulge you and your new family. Your nearest and dearest will want to share this happy time so put a little thought into what their budget might be so that if they ask you what you'd like, you've had a chance to come up with some ideas.

The basic layette

A 'layette' is a collection of clothing for a newborn child. A 'layette set' is a term that can be used to describe a gift of a set of clothing for a newborn. These days the term can encompass all essential newborn clothes and bedding.

Everyone likes something new to dress their infant in – especially when leaving hospital or receiving visitors for the first time. Just don't go mad. The main supermarkets do great value babygro/body packs for about £5, which are ideal as a first layer. On top of that your child will need:

- □ A few tops
- □ Baby cardigan
- □ Trousers
- □ Socks
- □ Winter babies will also need hats

Basic kit for birth to three months is probably three day outfits and three sleepsuits. Friends and family may add to this. The more you have, the less washing you need to do. Some babies could get through this many clothes in one day alone.

For night time most babies sleep in sleepsuits. Supermarkets offer good value sleepsuits in packs of three or four, which is all your child will need. Similarly for sleeping, your baby will need two sets of bedding (one to use while the other is being washed). Whether you opt for baby blankets or baby sleeping bags is entirely up to you. However, sleeping bags come in different sizes and so they will need to be replaced as your children grow, whereas blankets will last (provided your child doesn't keep kicking them off!).

Anything else you choose is **nice-to-have**, not **need-to-have**.

As your infant grows you will get a better idea of how you work around your child and what his or her needs will be. That is when you can make seasoned purchases on eBay or value-for-money finds in charity shops, or even snap up a bargain at a car boot sale or on Freecycle.

OTHER CLOTHES

This is where old school friends, neighbours, colleagues and family come into their own. Whether or not they're invited to, they will 'choose something nice for the baby' and usually buy it in size birth to three months.

TOP TIP: KEEP CLOTHING GIFTS WITH THE LABELS ATTACHED

Whenever someone buys your child a clothing gift, keep it safe WITH THE LABELS AND TAGS STILL ATTACHED. It is almost certain that your newborn will be inundated with clothes aged birth to three months but have little of anything else. Babies grow fast, so only cut labels off clothes as your child wears them. As you get used to your baby and how many clothes you really need in that size you can take the unworn items back to their shops and exchange them for seasonally appropriate clothes in bigger sizes. Baby Gap, M&S and Mothercare all have good, flexible returns policies.

If someone tells you they are thinking of buying an outfit for the baby and asks you for advice, ask them to get a bigger size. Opt for three to six months, six to 12 months or even 12–18 months. You are likely to get more baby-sized clothes than you need and yet have to go shopping for complete new wardrobes for later years.

Non-essential kit

There is so much kit and caboodle around, this chapter has really only focussed on the essential items. However, given how much has been omitted it is worth looking at those items that can be avoided. However, as with all aspects of parenting, everyone does it differently and what might work for one family will be a complete waste of money for another.

Extra rear view mirror for the car (to view your baby while driving)
They don't stick to the window properly and it could be argued that they

distract from the more important job of driving. If you want to check on your baby, pull over in a safe spot and give them your undivided attention.

Baby bath

Baby baths (which sit atop your existing bath) are nice-to-have items, not need-to-have. If the rim of your bath is narrow and abuts the wall, the baby bath might not even balance on top of your bath safely anyway. Baby support sponges allow your infant to have a bath in your normal bath for a fraction of the price.

As with all items of baby kit, the baby bath is a great example of why one parent's great bargain is another one's waste of money.

> ❝ Biggest waste of money we ever spent was on a baby bath. Who uses them? When they are very little you use the sink and then when they're bigger you use the bath. Baby bath! Who thought that one up? ❞
>
> Caroline, mum to Ben

> ❝ We used our baby bath for about a year. So quick to fill and uses much less water. The baby can hold on to the sides to steady themselves too. Oh, and our baby bath is 38 years old! ❞
>
> Catherine, mum to Annabel and Harry

Moses baskets for twins

Most babies love Moses baskets. Twins, on the whole, don't. They are so used to being in close contact with one another that suddenly separating your infants into their own beds is quite traumatic. Instead, place them side to side, facing each other in a regular cot. They'll much prefer it.

Wipe warmers

Honestly!

Bottle warmers

These were the second most-regretted baby purchase, according to 1,500 parents surveyed by infant milk formula manufacturer SMA Nutrition. Warm up your baby's milk by placing it under hot running water instead.

Baby carriers

These were voted *the* most regretted purchase. Those who got on with the carriers (such as BabyBjörn slings) used them relentlessly. Those who didn't get on with them, and bought them new, felt as if they'd wasted £50–£100. If you want a carrier, try and find one secondhand.

Bath thermometer

In the old days, parents used their elbows to judge water temperature. I still had a pair of elbows when I last looked!

Wet wipes for newborns

Newborns have very sensitive skin. Nappy changing is best done with cotton wool and warm water, not with chemical-laden (and expensive) wet wipes. Save them for when you're out and about.

Baby shoes

They're fiddly and your child will most likely kick them off. Stick to socks.

The definitive list for baby's first three months

Quite honestly, planning for the first three months of your newborn's life is quite enough.

Item	Sensible price	Where to source
Car seat	£45	Own brand combination seat from Mothercare
Cot mattress	£30	New via eBay
Pram/travel system	£50	School fete/church sale/charity shop/eBay
Moses basket	£10	Charity shop
Cot	£20	Charity shop/school newsletter
Sleep suits and baby bodies	Two packs for £10	New from supermarket
Steam steriliser	£0–£5	Freecycle, NCT sale or charity shop
Muslin squares	£7	Mothercare had a 50 pack of top-and-tail squares for £7

Baby bottles	£6	Kiddicare.com had the best value bottles when I looked but different sites have different offers all the time.
New bottle teats	£9 for six	Always buy these new!
Baby bouncer	£5	A great charity shop or NCT sale find
Toys & books	£5 the lot	Freecycle, car boot sales, jumble sales and school fetes are top locations to grab toy & book bargains
Baby sling (optional)	£15	NCT sale or charity shop
Essential baby clothes	£5	Freecycle or car boot sales

Total cost of kitting out baby: £222
Amount covered by the government's Health in Pregnancy Grant: £190
Amount new parents have to fund: £32

NB: These prices should act as a rough guide to sourcing secondhand baby kit and shopping around for the cheapest deals. Sometimes the bill can come to less; sometimes it will be considerably more.

The power of the Health in Pregnancy Grant

At the moment (that is, at the time of writing this chapter) all mothers-to-be are entitled to apply for a Health in Pregnancy Grant worth £190. This money is non-means tested and is available from the 25th week of pregnancy. For more information see page 42.

For now, it means parents can kit their child out in everything except nappies and (if required) infant milk formula for £32. That is starting to sound a lot more reasonable than the £1,560 the average mother spent three years ago.

This assumes friends, neighbours, work colleagues, and family etc haven't gifted anything to you.

All that new kit for your baby for just a £32 outlay from you and your partner. Bargain!

2. Planning for your new family

Once you have got over the shock or surprise of getting pregnant, you'll now have to work out how you are going to manage your new life as a parent. There is a lot to think about. Many parents will wonder how on earth they can pay all the bills AND manage childcare costs AND hold down a job. Others will be wondering how everything can be fitted into 24 measly little hours each day (the answer is simple: sleep is optional for the first three years!).

Whoever you are, and whether this pregnancy has been much planned and anticipated or a complete surprise, there is a lot to consider.

Statutory leave and allowances

Before working out how to manage your new life around your new baby, you first need to know what is possible.

EMPLOYED MOTHERS

If you are a mother who is an employee you are entitled to a minimum amount of time off work called **Statutory Leave**. This has been set by the government at 52 weeks.

- □ 26 weeks of *Ordinary Maternity Leave*, and
- □ 26 weeks of *Additional Maternity Leave*.

Statutory Maternity Pay

Statutory Maternity Pay (or SMP) is the minimum amount you can expect to receive while on maternity leave. However, in order to qualify, you must have been employed by the same employer without a break for at least 26 weeks by the time you are 24 weeks pregnant.

(For those who need more small-print, if you started work mid-week or your 24th week falls in the middle of a week, it will count as a complete week for the purposes of this calculation.)

You must also be earning at least the lower earnings limit for national insurance contributions – currently £95 a week.

So long as you can tick all those boxes then you can expect to get at least:

- □ 90% of your average weekly earnings for the first 6 weeks of maternity leave
- □ The lower of either £123.06 a week or 90% of those weekly earnings for the next 33 weeks
- □ In total, qualifying employees get SMP for 39 weeks

Some employers are more generous. For example, there are companies that pay your full salary for 26 weeks before dropping down to the statutory minimum; others pay even more.

TOP TIP: USE YOUR HOLIDAY TO BOOST LEAVE

Squeeze another month's leave on full pay – use your holiday. While you're on maternity leave, some companies allow you to accrue your annual holiday and add it on to the start or end of your maternity leave. Check your company's terms to see if you can do this. It could give you another four week's leave on full pay which is not to be sniffed at!

Expectant mums need to check their contract of employment or ask their Human Resources department at work for details of their company's maternity scheme.

Inform the right people at the right time in the right way

In order to make sure you qualify for everything to which you're entitled, it is important to inform the right people at the right time, in the right way. So, here's a list of just who you need to tell and when.

1. **Tell your employer you're pregnant**

    Your employer should be told about your pregnancy no later than the 23rd week of pregnancy. Many employees tell their boss once they are safely over the 12-week point or when they have had their first scan.

2. **Inform your employer of your planned leaving date**

    By the 23rd week of pregnancy you should also inform your employer of your planned date for stopping work. This can be whenever you like from the 28th week of pregnancy. Most mothers try and maximise the amount of leave they have after the baby is born to make their SMP stretch as far as possible. Don't worry if you say one thing now and another later. You are entitled to change your mind, provided you give your employer 28 days' notice.

3. **Give your boss the right paperwork**

    I'm referring to the precious **MATB1 form**. This form simply confirms when your baby is due and will be given to you by your doctor or midwife in your third trimester (around the 28th week of pregnancy). The MATB1 needs to be handed to your employer as soon as you get it (by all means take a copy first!) – you will not be given SMP without it.

4. **Contact with work while on leave**

    Once you're on maternity leave your employer can continue to contact you (provided it's not unreasonable).

TOP TIP: WORKING WHILE ON LEAVE

You can do some work during maternity leave, so long as it is not more than 10 days. This could come in handy as a way of earning extra pennies. It could also ease your path back to work.

- You might consider doing one day a week from home in the last 10 weeks of your planned leave, if that works for your boss too.
- It could give you the chance to settle your baby into a routine away from you by doing two days a week for the last five weeks of your leave (if you're thinking of returning on a more full-time basis).
- You could do four hours a week for nearly five months to give you a little more money in the latter (poorer) stages of your maternity leave to make it easier to pay the bills.

All this depends on the work you do, how practical it is to keep doing something and how willing your boss and your colleagues are to you working in this way. There is no obligation on either party to enable this to happen. If it is inconvenient for either the employer or the employee (or colleagues) then no one can force the issue.

---

5. **Returning to work**

   You should have informed your employer of your planned return date before heading off on maternity leave. After all, your company might need to hire a temporary member of staff to cover your role while you're away. However, that date is not set in stone. If you want to return to work earlier or later than planned, that is absolutely fine, *provided you've given your employer at least eight weeks' notice of your new intended return date.*

6. **A word of warning**

   Some employers may be more generous when it comes to paying Statutory Maternity Pay but they don't do this out of the goodness of their hearts: they do it because they want you back. It costs a lot to recruit and train someone, so if you are planning not to return to work, make sure you go through both your contract of employment and the details of your maternity benefit with a fine tooth comb – you might have to pay some of your maternity benefit back if you don't return to work for a set period of time.

EMPLOYED FATHERS

Statutory Paternity Leave

Employed fathers are entitled to Statutory Paternity Leave for two weeks after their child is born. They too must have been employed for at least 26 weeks by their employer by the time of the 24th week of pregnancy.

However 'dad' doesn't have to mean biological father. Statutory Paternity Leave can be claimed by:

- ◻ The biological father, or
- ◻ The mother's partner. That includes partners in same-sex relationships.

The proviso is that the partner will be fully involved in the child's upbringing and will be taking the time off to support the mother or care for the baby.

To qualify for pay, 'fathers' must earn at least the lower earnings limit for National Insurance Contributions (currently £95 a week). If not, they are only entitled to unpaid paternity leave. However, they could get Income Support while on paternity leave if this is the case.

Statutory Paternity Pay is paid at a rate of:

- ◻ £123.06 a week, or
- ◻ 90% of your average weekly earnings, whichever is less.

If fathers or partners don't qualify, there is nothing to be lost and everything to be gained by having a conversation with the employer, who may just give them some time off. Of course, fathers can always take paid holiday.

At the time of writing, proposals had been put forward to increase paid paternity leave so it's worth checking for the most up-to-date legislation.

How paternity leave can be taken

As with everything else involving parental leave, there are rules governing how this leave can be taken.

- ◻ It cannot be taken as odd days.
- ◻ Dads can take either one week or two weeks but they must be taken together.
- ◻ Dads can choose to start the leave either on the day the baby is born, a number of days or weeks after the baby is born, or

from a specific date after the first day of the week in which the baby is expected to be born.

□ The leave can start on any day of the week but it has to finish within 56 days of the baby being born.

As with mothers, some employers offer fathers more generous schemes than the statutory government terms allow. It is therefore worthwhile for expectants dads to check their benefits.

Tax credits and other allowances

Once the baby is born, family finances will be tested like never before. Unless you decide to have siblings for your baby, your finances will not undergo such tumultuous change like this for a while. Therefore it is important to know whether you are entitled to any means-tested benefits to ease the burden of raising your family.

HEALTH/WEALTH WARNING

This chapter was written before the general election. At the time, there was no intended shake-up of the benefit system. However, the country is facing public sector borrowing on an unprecedented level. It is highly likely that benefits will not continue without some amendments. Therefore, check whether you are still eligible for any of the following:

• Working Tax Credit
• Child Tax Credit
• Family Benefit
• Health in Pregnancy Grant
• Child Trust Fund

Also check whether they are still available under the same terms (details below).

BENEFITS FOR ALL
(NON-MEANS-TESTED BENEFITS)

Parenthood is an expensive business. All the political parties recognise this and there are a variety of financial measures designed to help families cope. Some of these are available to everybody; some aren't.

All these benefits cost money and whichever Government has to untangle the country's borrowing after the election will be looking to cut expenditure.

□ It is possible that Child Trust Funds will be phased out completely or only offered on a means-tested basis.

□ The Health in Pregnancy Grant may become means tested or phased out completely.

□ Child Benefit is longer established and could lose more votes but it could also become means tested.

□ Working Tax Credits and Child Tax Credits may not be offered to as many families as they are now.

So, the sooner you can grab your entitlement and secure it for your children, the better off your family will be.

Here are the benefits that are available to everyone.

The Health in Pregnancy Grant

□ All expectant mothers are entitled to a grant worth £190, which the government will pay directly into your bank or building society account.

□ It could help buy vital items for your baby such as a new car seat or cot mattress (see Buying new for your newborn, page 10).

□ As with other government grants, it is not paid automatically: you have to apply.

□ Expectant mothers have to be at least 25 weeks pregnant and have to have been given health advice from a midwife or doctor to help both mother and baby stay healthy during pregnancy.

□ Claim forms are only available from midwives or doctors (whoever you see for your antenatal appointments).

□ They usually give expectant mums the claim form at the next antenatal appointment after the 25th week of pregnancy.

□ The health professional needs to sign and complete their part of the form before giving it to you.

Go to www.direct.gov.uk/money4mum2be for more information.

Free prescriptions and dental treatment

Mums are also entitled to free medical prescriptions and dental treatment from the start of their pregnancy through to the child's first birthday.

This is done automatically.

Child Benefit

At the moment, the primary carers of all children receive Child Benefit, regardless of how much they earn. This is paid directly into the carer's bank account at a rate of £20.30 a week for the first (or only) child and £13.40 per week for each subsequent child.

Child Benefit is generally paid four-weekly but can be paid weekly to those on Income Support, income-based Jobseeker's Allowance, income related Employment and Support Allowance or to single parents.

Many parents will rely on this money to make ends meet. It is enough to pay for nappies, wipes, baby or child clothes, basic foodstuffs and other necessities (see page 34).

For those who can survive without dipping in to this benefit, it provides the perfect opportunity to build up a vital nest egg for your child.

TOP TIP: SAVE LITTLE AND OFTEN

Saving just £20 each month means you will have put aside nearly £4,000 (£3,840) by your child's 16th birthday – and that's before interest has been added. Figures from Nationwide estimate that if you put £20 of Child Benefit aside each month until your child's 16th birthday you would have collected £4,100 with accrued interest.

(Based on Nationwide's Smart account, with rates correct as at January 2010. As interest rates rise, that money will grow. Whether it grows in real terms is another matter.)

There is no end to what the money might be useful for. One thing is for certain: *your child's financial needs will grow as they do,* so if you have the opportunity to save some of that Child Benefit, grab it with both hands.

APPLY EARLY!

The only way to get Child Benefit is to fill in the form and send it, along with your child's birth or adoption certificate, to the Child Benefit Office. Forms are available:

- In the Bounty pack given to new parents in hospital, or
- Online via the website. Print off, fill in and return the online form.

For more information contact the Child Benefit Helpline on 0845 302 1444, textphone 0845 302 1474 or visit the website: http://www.direct.gov.uk/en/MoneyTaxAndBenefits/TaxCreditsandChildBenefit/Childbenefits/index.htm

Child Trust Fund

At the moment, all children are eligible to receive at least £250 from the government, to be paid directly into a tax-free Child Trust Fund account. The account belongs to them, not to you, and the money cannot be touched until they are 18 years old. Children from lower income families will receive £500.

At the moment, the government has said it will top that amount up with a further payment of £250 when children turn seven years old (£500 for children from lower income families).

The idea is that parents, other family members and friends can contribute to this savings account to the tune of £1,200 a year tax-free. You get to choose whether you want that money put into a regular savings-type account or into a stock market-backed investment. The latter is the government's preferred vehicle as it gives the greatest chance for the money to grow but, with savings accounts, what you see is what you get.

Pros:

- Savings are tax free.
- Families can accumulate more than £22,000 net of interest or capital growth over 18 years.
- That could build a pot worth more than £30,000 if invested in an equity-based option.
- Those saving just £20 a month could build a pot worth nearly £6,000*.

□ It could be used to help fund university, buy a car, fund an apprenticeship, put a deposit down on a property etc.

*Figures from Nationwide based on saving £20 a month into a cash CTF until child reaches age 18. Total sum on maturity would be £5,921, based on a child born in January 2010 and assuming interest rates remain at their current levels.

Cons:

□ Politicians are already talking about scrapping the £250 payment for seven year olds.

□ Child Trust Funds may be phased out altogether for all but the poorest children.

□ The child gains the money at 18 with no parental controls. So you could watch in horror as your child blows the lot on a super-charged gap year.

□ Once invested, the money cannot be touched except by the child when they reach adulthood.

□ Some parents have said they found the system over-complicated and therefore off-putting.

There is good news for even the most confused parents though. Even if you invested none of your own money into the Child Trust Fund and just put the £250 aside, followed by the same again when your child is aged seven, Nationwide estimates that money would grow to £856. Ok, so it won't go very far but why would you turn down the opportunity to give your child a bit of financial help?

GETTING A CHILD TRUST FUND STARTED

- You will receive a Child Trust Fund information pack once your baby is born.
- It is up to you whether you choose a cash savings account or a stocks and shares account.
- If you do not choose the government will open an account in your child's name and put £250 into it.

For more information, visit the Child Trust Fund website at http://www. childtrustfund.gov.uk/.

TOP TIP: YOUR CHILD'S FINANCIAL NEEDS GROW WITH YOUR CHILD

Whatever your financial decision-making, always remember the first money rule of parenting.

You might think your baby is going to be expensive but never forget: **your child's financial needs will grow as your child grows.** Put as much aside as you can now and when your child is small. You'll need it later!

MEANS-TESTED BENEFITS

Raising a family is an expensive business. There are allowances that can help but they are not paid automatically to needy parents. Parents have to know what they are entitled to and how to apply. What's more, the system is naturally complicated so there is no way of writing a one-rule-suits-all approach here.

The good news is families don't have to suffer utter penury before they qualify.

At the moment, households with incomes of around £66,000 may still qualify for some financial assistance. That is likely to change to households with incomes of less than £50,000 in the future but it is still providing some kind of help where it is needed.

The bad news is that it is up to the individual to apply – and reapply each year and keep on top of any changes as they occur – in order to get and maintain those benefits and avoid the nightmare of over or underpayments.

Working Tax Credit

Working Tax Credit tops up the earnings of lower paid workers and workers with a disability. The amount you receive is based on your circumstances. The basic threshold for those without children aged over 25 and working at least 30 hours a week is £13,253 for individuals and £18,023 for couples.

If you are part of a couple the Working Tax Credit will be paid to the working party.

> □ Those with children can still be eligible for Working Tax Credit if they earn more than the threshold, provided they are at least 16 years old and work at least 16 hours a week.

□ There is a childcare element to the working tax credit that can be worth up to £175 per week for one child or £300 for two or more children. That element of the benefit is paid to the primary carer.

□ Those eligible for Working Tax Credit that have to pay for childcare may be eligible for help in meeting those costs.

What you get

Working Tax Credit	
Working Tax Credit elements	**Maximum amount paid for 2010–2011**
Basic element – one per single claimant or couple	£1,920
Couples' and lone parents' element (paid in addition to the basic element but only one Couples' element allowed per couple)	£1,890
30 hour element (paid if you work 30 hours or more per week but only one element allowed per couple)	£790
Disabled worker element (a couple can receive two elements if both claimants are eligible)	£2,570
Severe disability element (a couple can receive two elements if both claimants are eligible)	£1,095
50+ return to work element (working 16-29 hours per week). Payable for up to 12 months	£1,320
50+ return to work element (working 30 hours or more). Payable for up to 12 months	£1,965
Childcare element, childcare for one child	80% of cost of childcare to a maximum of £140 a week
Childcare element, childcare for two or more children	80% of cost of childcare to a maximum of £240 a week

(Source: Which?)

Child/Family Tax Credit

□ This offers additional support for families with children.

□ Parents don't have to be working to be eligible.

□ Incredibly, 90% of families are eligible for some kind of financial support through this system.

□ The amount you receive depends upon your income (or joint income if you are part of a couple).

    □ A higher rate is paid to families with children under a year old.

    □ It can be claimed right through your child's life until the 1st of September after they turn 16 years old. If you are only eligible for Child Tax Credit you cannot claim for help with childcare payments.

What you get

The Child Tax Credit is made up of many different elements. Some people are eligible for many different elements; others just for one or two. The maximum entitlement for each element is detailed below.

Child Tax Credit	
Child Tax Credit elements	**Maximum amount paid for 2010–2011**
Family element – the basic element for families responsible for one or more children	£545
Extra Family element paid to families with one or more children under the age of one. Only one payment is made even if you have more than one child under one	£545
Child element – one for each child or young person you are responsible for	£2,300
Disability element – one for each child you are responsible for if you are receiving Disability Living Allowance for the child, or the child is registered blind or has been taken off the blind register in the 28 weeks before the date of claim	£2,715
Severe disability element – one for each child you are responsible for if you receive the Highest Rate Care Component of Disability Living Allowance for the child	£1,095

(Source: Which?)

The following table breaks down, by broad salary bands, what you and your family may be entitled to receive in Child Tax Credit if you do not qualify for Working Tax Credit

Child Tax Credit 2009–2010			
Household income	One Child	Two Children	Three Children
Less than £16,040	£2,785	£5,022	£7,260
£20,000	£1,240	£3,259	£5,715
£25,000	£545	£1,309	£3,765
£30,000	£545	£545	£1,815
£35,000	£545	£545	£545
£40,000	£545	£545	£545
£45,000	£545	£545	£545
£50,000	£545	£545	£545
£55,000	£210	£210	£210
£60,000	n/a	n/a	n/a

(Source: Which?)

You can choose whether you receive Working Tax Credit or Child Tax Credit weekly or four weekly. The money can either be paid directly into your bank account or you can receive it from the Post Office. Application packs for Tax Credits are available via the Tax Credit Helpline at 0845 300 3900.

GETTING STARTED

- For more information on whether you are eligible to receive these and other benefits, visit the Inland Revenue website at **http://www.hmrc.gov.uk/ taxcredits/index.htm**.
- It will guide you through a series of questions to determine your basic eligibility.
- Alternatively, visit **www.entitledto.co.uk**.
- This independent website has an online calculator which will do the hard work for you and save you trawling through the government's own (slower) assessment process.

www.entitled.co.uk may also show you whether you are entitled to claim other benefits, such as Council Tax and Housing Benefit.

The costs of raising a disabled child

When parents first discover that their child has a disability, the first thing they think about is certainly not money.

Most parents, faced with the knowledge that their beautiful son or daughter has a serious and disabling condition, are just concerned about how they are going to raise their child and what they need to know about his or her condition in order to manage day-to-day care.

Over time, these concerns broaden to incorporate how to manage to raise healthy siblings alongside a disabled child without the needs of the siblings being completely overshadowed; how to juggle work and full-time caring responsibilities; how to get much needed childcare support or respite care; how to go out and about; seeking appropriate needs-based education for that child; and what the future might hold for that child as they become a disabled adult.

However, although it is only right that the day-to-day practicalities of raising a disabled child should dominate a parent's thoughts, it is vital that parents know just what the financial implications are and where to get help.

> ## A SURVEY CONDUCTED BY THE TRUE COLOURS TRUST IN 2004 REVEALED THAT:
> **55% of families with a disabled child live on the poverty line, primarily because of the costs of raising a disabled child.**

In 2007, the Every Disabled Child Matters campaign, which was an alliance of Mencap, Contact a Family, the Council for Disabled Children and the Special Educational Consortium, was still fighting for better financial support for parents of disabled children.

The campaign's findings make sobering reading:

- 93% of families reported some form of financial difficulty.
- More than one in five families with disabled children cannot afford to feed their children properly.

    □ Such families are 50% more likely to be in debt than others and 50% less likely to be able to afford new clothes or school outings compared with other families.

Some, but not all, of this poverty could be avoidable, because only 50% of parents of disabled children were claiming the full allowances to which they were entitled.

EXTRA SAVINGS HELP

From April 2010, disabled children will receive an annual government contribution of £100 paid directly into their Child Trust Fund. The most severely disabled children will receive £200 a year. Payments will be made to those children entitled to receive money under the Disability Living Allowance. The government has done this to help put extra resources aside to help meet the financial needs of today's disabled children as they reach adulthood.

MAKING A CLAIM

There are three main elements of financial support from which parents of a disabled child might be eligible to make a claim. They are:

    □ The disability living allowance
    □ The carer's allowance
    □ The disabled child element of child tax credits

Disability Living Allowance

The disability living allowance has two elements to it: the care component and the mobility component.

Basically, in order to get some form of allowance, your child must need a lot more supervision than other children of the same age. Unless your child is severely ill and unlikely to live for very long, no benefit will be paid until after your child is three months old.

There is detailed information on whether you might be eligible to receive Disability Living Allowance on the government website **www.direct.gov.uk**.

As the Disability Living Allowance is in two parts – the care component and the mobility component – you may be able to get just one component or both.

The allowance is paid at different rates, according to the severity of disability and how it affects day-to-day living.

Care component	Weekly rate
Highest rate	£70.35
Middle rate	£47.10
Lowest rate	£18.65
Mobility component	**Weekly rate**
Higher rate	£49.10
Lower rate	£18.65

Your individual circumstances will affect how much you can get.

(Source: www.direct.gov.uk)

Carer's Allowance

The Carer's Allowance can be paid to you if you are aged over 16 and spend at least 35 hours a week caring for someone who is disabled. You will only receive this if the person you are caring for is receiving Disability Living Allowance at the middle or highest rate for personal care. If you share the duty of care with another person, only one of you will receive the allowance.

You cannot get a Carer's Allowance if you earn more than £95 a week after expenses.

Disabled element of Child Tax Credits

The amount of extra tax credits you may receive depends upon how much extra care your child needs. In the 2009/2010 tax year this was assessed as:

- □ £2,670 a year – around £51 a week – if your child is disabled
- □ £3,745 a year – around £72 a week – if your child is severely disabled
- □ Disability Living Allowance doesn't count as income when your tax credits are worked out

START THE BALL ROLLING

1. Phone the Benefit Enquiry Line to get an application pack sent out to you (0800 88 22 00).

2. Download an application form through the benefits online service at www.dwp.gov.uk/eservice.

3. Check your eligibility to claim at www.direct.gov.uk/en/DisabledPeople/FinancialSupport/ DisabilityLivingAllowance.

If you want someone to help you through the benefits maze and direct you to other support agencies, contact the Citizens Advice Bureau at www.citizensadvice.org.uk.

Where those extra costs lurk

Writing in the *Guardian* in February 2009, Dea Birkett painted a stark picture of just why day-to-day living costs so much more for a disabled child than an able-bodied sibling. Here are some of the costs she listed:

- Bike for my disabled daughter **£795**; bike for her siblings **£79.95**
- Childcare costs for my disabled daughter **£250 per week**; childcare if we could use a childminder for all three children **£100 per week**
- Cost to get to cinema for my disabled daughter, **£6** in accessible taxi; cost to get to cinema for siblings **£0** with free transport on bus
- Cost of adaptations to house **£20,000**
- Cost of new wheelchair-accessible car **£18,000**; cost of our old car **£1,000**
- Cost of large-print edition of *Great Expectations* for her English GCSE **£35**; cost of school books for siblings **£0**
- Cost of wheelchair repairs, approx **£70 per month**
- Cost of trip to Paris on Eurostar sitting together as family of five **£600+**; cost of travelling by Eurostar to Paris if we didn't have a disabled child **£295**

> ◻ Loss of income due to having to attend multiple
> appointments: immeasurable

(Source: Dea Birkett, Copyright Guardian News & Media Ltd 2009)

WHERE TO GO FOR HELP

One of the biggest issues that parents of disabled children face is the feeling of isolation. Parents can sometimes not know of other parents and children in a similar position but might desperately need either reassurance or the knowledge from someone who's been there before them of what comes next and how they're going to cope.

Luckily, there are some fantastic support groups that can help parents, the children themselves, and any siblings. Here are just a few of the many, fantastic organisations out there that could really make a difference:

- ◻ **Child Disability Help**. This group aims to provide support to families in the UK with a child or children under the age of 16 with a disability (**www.child-disability.co.uk**).
- ◻ **Whizz-kidz**. Provides help to disabled children and young people, from customised mobility scooters and other vehicles, to training, advice and life skills (**www.whizz-kidz.org.uk/ gethelp**).
- ◻ **Family Fund**. The Family Fund gives grants for things that would help to make life easier for families with a disabled child. Last year, it helped around 50,000 UK families with grants of £30.5 million (**www.familyfund.org.uk**).
- ◻ **Contact a Family**. A UK-wide charity providing advice, information and support for the parents of disabled children. It can help you find local support groups in your area as well as vital help and information on your child's condition, allowances and day-to-day issues (**www.cafamily.org.uk**).

❝ Great Ormond Street Hospital is looking into the financial implications of having a chronically ill child. We certainly found the expense of buying allergy-friendly food, such as different milks and snacks etc, was HUGE. I have often commented on how difficult it can be for some families. Imagine that for every party your children are invited to you have to provide your own child's party tea, complete with home-made iced cake. Even infant formula for children on a restrictive diet is more expensive. So-called cheap food goods like sausages are often ones you can't opt for. It is often only the ones that are organic and posh that are OK for all the allergies. I know our kids have a healthy diet and we've managed all of this, but for many families this may not be an option. ❞

Michelle, mum to Molly and George

3. Family costs and affording childcare

Getting the budget to balance

Looking at government allowances and benefits is only half the equation. It might seem a long way off, but before you have time to draw breath, that little bump will turn into a walking talking bundle of expense. Even if you spend little or no more on housing and food there is what economists might call the 'opportunity cost' of having that child in the first place.

For example, even if you return to work full-time, you will have to pay for childcare; you might not be able to travel as much as your employer or you had assumed; you may no longer be willing to take the unsavoury shifts at work; or you might be forced to do so in order that you and your partner can juggle childcare while still being able to afford to pay the bills.

TOP TIP: NOTE EVERY EXPENSE, NO MATTER HOW SMALL

Even if you try to avoid spending any more, your child will make sure that you do.

HERE IT IS, IN BLACK AND WHITE

- Figures from the Office of National Statistics (ONS) showed that, in 2008, the average family of two adults and two children spent around £690 a week.
- That figure includes everything: food, drink, housing, transport, clothes, leisure, fuel, phone bills and restaurants.
- It equates to an annual spend of £35,880.
- To have that much to spend, a family must first have earned more than £50,000 in gross salary terms.
- That also assumes you have all the pension provisions you could want or need; you've saved enough to renew the car etc and don't need to put anything aside on top of that.

Now add in loss of earnings from one parent and/or the cost of childcare.

In other words, you are now entering THE most expensive phase of your life.

It is ironic that, at a time when you may well need to work less and therefore earn less, your household expenditure could rocket. This is where it pays to understand the dynamics of family finances and the implications any one decision may have on the entire family budget.

> ❝ I have always saved in a variety of ways. One method I use is to 'tax' myself. So, each time I take money out of the cash point, I deduct 10% and put it somewhere safe. To my brain, I've still taken out the same amount of spending money; I just have to make that money work a bit harder. At the same time, I've got a savings pot of money building up ready for birthdays or special occasions such as family meals out. ❞
>
> Roger, dad to Chris and James

To work or not to work

While you will undoubtedly re-visit this issue many times during your child's life, whether to return to work full-time, part-time, or not at all first rears its head in pregnancy. To decide, it is not enough to look at current income and out-goings, you must weigh up the cost and availability of childcare and the impact each childcare choice might have on your working life.

NURSERY FEES

The typical cost of a full-time nursery place for a child under 2 is:

* £176 a week in England – more than £9,000 a year.
* £168 in Scotland
* £156 in Wales
* £425 in London
* £218 in the South East of England

In some parts of the country that cost can exceed £20,000 a year

(Source: Daycare Trust Childcare Cost Survey)

Unless you have family living nearby, there are three main childcare options when your baby is small: nursery, childminders and nannies. Whatever you decide, if you do opt for to use childcare, make sure you use **Childcare Vouchers**, if possible. Most employers now offer them and most childcare facilities accept them.

CHILDCARE VOUCHERS

In the not so old days, childcare cost even more than it does now because cash-strapped families had to find a way of funding these costs out of their net salary. This was ridiculous. It meant those employing a nanny, for example, had to first pay tax on their earnings, then pay employers' tax and National Insurance out of their net salary and then pay the nanny, who also paid tax and National Insurance.

Thank goodness times have now changed. Employees can opt to take childcare vouchers in lieu of part of their salary, which means they don't pay tax on that element of their earnings. The savings per person can be as much as £1,195 a year in tax and National Insurance.

It is important to find out if your partner's employer also offers childcare vouchers. Both parents can claim and this could add up to a combined tax and National Insurance saving of £2,391.

Childcare vouchers can only be used to pay for a type of childcare that is Ofsted registered and also registered to accept vouchers. All nurseries and childminders are regularly inspected by Ofsted. Remember though that Ofsted only operates in England. Scotland, Northern Ireland and Wales have their own inspection bodies with whom you should check about childcare in those areas. For the past three years, nannies have also had the opportunity to voluntarily register on the Ofsted Childcare Register. Those who have may also have part of their salary paid by you in vouchers. This makes registered nannies more attractive to employers as they are cheaper and they go through the same checks as other childcare facilities.

TOP TIP: ASK ABOUT CHILDCARE VOUCHERS

Make sure you and your partner ask your employers about their childcare voucher scheme early on, and check that your childcare option of choice accepts childcare vouchers. It makes a big difference to the family finances. For more information visit **www.direct.gov.uk**.

Childcare options

NURSERY

Pros:

- Your child will be looked after by a team of qualified individuals.
- There will be other children to play with.
- Many offer extra-curricular lessons such as music, computers for tots and even swimming that they arrange and supervise.
- Some arrange trips to keep your child stimulated and to provide a variety of learning environments.
- Exposure to other children can build up your child's immune system.
- Some offer a reduction in fees for second and subsequent children.
- If a member of staff is ill, your child will still be looked after – it is up to the nursery to arrange suitable care.
- Nurseries are inspected by Ofsted so you can read past inspections and, just as with any school, get a feel for the strengths and weaknesses of any facility. You can also take

some comfort that Ofsted's checking procedure should ensure an acceptable minimum standard of care.

Cons:

- Nursery workers can be poorly paid and staff turnover can be high.
- In urban environments the opportunities for outside play can be small.
- Most nurseries only cater for parents working Monday to Friday in office hours.
- If your child is ill, they don't go to nursery and you don't go to work.
- Exposure to lots of children can mean lots of new illness – not to mention head lice!
- Sometimes staff morale is low, not all staff are trained to the highest level and supervision may not be set at the levels the nursery has promised.
- Children can be left to their own devices if they are either too quiet or too challenging.

TYPICAL COSTS FOR NURSERIES

- The average full-time nursery cost for a child under the age of two is £176 a week in England.
- Parents in London and the South East are most likely to pay more. The average cost for a full-time place for under twos rises to £218 per week.
- Most nurseries charge for the days your child is set to attend, not the days they actually attend. So, if your child is ill and is excluded from nursery, you will still pay, whether or not you work that day.
- The average annual expenditure across England for a child under the age of two attending nursery full-time is nearly £10,000 a year (£9,152)

(Source: Daycare Trust Childcare cost survey)

Note: Many parents I spoke to have paid far more for nursery places in some smart London commuter towns. It is not unusual for them to fork out between £50 and £75 a day: that's £250–£375 a week.

Parents in London face paying up to £22,100 for 50 hours childcare a week. **That's more expensive than private school fees**.

CHILDMINDERS

Pros:

- Many children like the security of the 'home from home' set-up a childminder provides.
- Many childminders have children of their own that provide instant playmates.
- Many childminders offer wrap-around childcare services for those at pre-school or school that can take the nightmare out of school hours and holidays and provide continuity of care.
- A smaller group of children can often mean either a wide variety of activities or activity more closely matched to their needs.
- Again, childminders are subject to Ofsted inspections; their results are published online and therefore subject to public (especially parental) scrutiny and an Ofsted inspection should guarantee an acceptable minimum standard of care.

Cons:

- Childminders look after many children, not just yours, so they may not have the flexibility to cope with other activities you want your child to undertake.
- There might be greater opportunities for outings or a wider variety of excursions but you will probably have to fund these on top of the day to day childcare costs.
- If your child is ill, the childminder may not be able to care for them (depending on the other children in their care at the time).
- If the childminder is ill, there may not be scope for any continuity of care – ie you don't go in to work. (In reality, some childminders act as emergency carers for one another and this can work well, but not all childminders offer this facility.)

TYPICAL COSTS FOR CHILDMINDERS

- The typical cost of a full-time under two's place is £166 per week.
- Childminders are self-employed, so you won't have to pay any tax on top of that fee.
- Some childminders charge a booking fee to secure your child's place, particularly in high demand areas, or those that have a link to particular schools.

The average annual cost across England for a child under two attending a childminder full-time is £8,632.

(Source: Daycare Trust Childcare cost survey)

Note: The parents I spoke to who contributed to this book showed just how much costs can vary. Their annual costs – had their children attended full-time – would have ranged from approximately £7,000 to nearly £20,000, depending on location.

NANNIES AND AU PAIRS

Pros:

- Your child is looked after in their own home.
- It costs no more for second and subsequent children – the cost of a nanny is the cost of a nanny.
- Activities are tailored to your child's needs.
- Everything can work around your child's existing routine.
- If your child is ill, the nanny can still look after them.
- As the employer, you get to agree when the suitable opportunities are for your nanny to take holiday days.
- You can nanny-share with friends, neighbours or just other parents in the area to save costs (see page 75 on cutting costs).
- Nannies can be employed on a live-in or a daily basis. If you have a decent sized spare room and other suitable facilities (eg an en-suite or room for a TV in the bedroom etc) then you might want to consider a live-in nanny. The overall costs are cheaper. Alternatively, for those who prefer their home to be

their own at the end of a long day, a daily nanny could be the answer. (Costs for both types detailed below.)

Cons:

- □ If you are the nanny's sole employer, your child may not meet up with many other children unless your nanny is quite gregarious.
- □ Without other non-family children to play with regularly, your child may take longer to adjust to a school environment and to learn to take turns and fit in with the routine of others.
- □ There may be extra costs you have to bear if you want your child to go out and about, from playgroups to day trips.
- □ You are the employer so you will need to recruit and interview.
- □ You will also need to draw up a contract of employment and pay employer's National Insurance contributions.
- □ If your nanny gets pregnant you will have to pay maternity benefits (although the government refunds these costs) and recruit a temporary nanny to cover the maternity period.
- □ Not all nannies are Ofsted registered, so some may cost more than others for the same level of take-home pay. Around half of the nannies surveyed by NannyTax for its annual pay survey were registered with Ofsted.
- □ Those who are not registered also don't get subjected to regular inspections that give you a third party assessment of the childcare your baby is receiving.

TYPICAL COSTS FOR NANNIES

The best way to lay these costs out is to look at average costs for both daily and live-in nannies in different geographical areas of Britain.

CENTRAL LONDON
Live-in nannies average £355 a week, equivalent to a gross annual salary of almost £24,000.

Daily nannies average £466 a week, equivalent to a gross annual salary of more than £32,000.

OUTER LONDON
Live-in nannies average £315 a week (or £21,000 per annum).
Daily nannies average £380 a week (£26,000pa).

OTHER TOWNS AND CITIES
Live-in nannies average £280 a week (£18,300pa).
Daily nannies average £332 a week (£22,220pa).

THE COUNTRYSIDE
Live-in nannies average £283 a week (£18,500pa).
Daily nannies average £321 a week (£21,400pa).

(Source: NannyTax annual wages survey 2009)

These weekly figures are what the nanny would receive net of tax and National Insurance. The annual figures are gross. Employers (ie you, the parents) would also have to pay employers' National Insurance.

Getting the hard work done for you

NannyTax (**www.nannytax.co.uk**) is an agency specifically set up to help manage your nanny's payroll issues. For an annual fee (currently £270), they can manage every element of your nanny's pay (other than actually paying it on your behalf!) and they also issue payslips. They can provide sample employment contracts which are a great starting point and can offer advice on recruiting a nanny.

Many nannies are registered with nanny agencies. For an annual, monthly or one-off fee, prospective employers (ie you, the parents) can register with those agencies, who will advertise your vacancy for you and screen their database of nannies to come up with a shortlist of candidates. All agencies are different yet they have one thing in common. They act as intermediaries in the same way as, say estate agents or recruitment consultants. If the relationship works you will find the agency saves you a lot of time and heartache and works very well for the money. If the relationship really doesn't work you may wonder what you're paying for as none of the shortlisted candidates fit your criteria or the agency doesn't seem to be meeting your needs in the way you expect.

TOP TIP: ASK LOCAL MUMS FOR RECOMMENDATIONS

Ask around other parents in the area or on local area chat forums to find out which agencies other parents would recommend and why. Word of mouth is invaluable to ensure you get the service you need.

How to choose the right childcare for you

Yes, cost will be a major consideration, but there is also the not insignificant matter of your child's welfare to consider.

COST IS NOT THE ONLY CONSIDERATION

Cost should not be the only consideration when looking at returning to work and what type of childcare to opt for. Take your child with you to look around a nursery or childminder's house and see how they react to the environment as well as how the child-caring professionals behave with your child.

Ask about feeding, routines, outings, variety, interaction with other children and whether the same staff look after particular age groups of children each day or whether staff are rotated. See how your child interacts with the other children within that environment.

Similarly, when interviewing nannies, have your child in the room. See how the nanny talks to your child and what interaction takes place while you're putting the kettle on. If you are thinking of nanny sharing, try and assess how your child interacts with other children in that nanny's care. After all, while you are at work, you will want to feel reassured that your child is receiving the best possible care.

Childcare for school-age children

Parents of pre-school age children are often under the misapprehension that the whole juggling act gets a whole lot easier once the children are safely ensconced in school six hours a day for five days a week. After all, that frees up a lot of time to make returning to work a more worthwhile option, right?

Not exactly.

Children aren't always in school for five days a week. During the first year of school (when children are in Reception) many are only at school for two and a half or three hours a day for the first term, which can play havoc with work schedules.

Holidays: half term and end of term holidays take up around 13 weeks a year. Employers usually only give their staff four or five weeks holidays a year. That either means parents spend a fortune on holiday clubs to cover the time when they're working, or they take holidays as a tag team, so they don't spend any time with each other but they do minimise the childcare costs during these endless breaks.

Other occasions: You will be required at school for: class assemblies, school concerts and nativity plays. There are ad hoc days when school is shut altogether – for example, most schools have at least one 'inset day' per term, where the teachers attend for training but the school is shut to the children.

Finally there are days when your child is ill and cannot go to school, or the school is shut because the boiler has broken (again), or the school day is radically different and you are needed to ferry your child to a different location at a different time because of school trips, sports days, inter-school competitions etc.

In short, juggling your career with your child's school career can be more challenging than juggling a career with nursery or a childminder because there are so many more variables involved. So, before you look at the exciting elements of your child's school career (buying the uniform, the friends he or she will make) you will have to re-assess childcare. It is worth re-visiting the decisions you made about work/life balance in light of the changes to your child's daily patterns?

Of course, there are many options available: breakfast clubs in schools, wrap-around care clubs affiliated to schools, childminders, even nannies and local nurseries that operate walking buses to their after-school facilities. The trick is in finding the option that's best for your child. In some cases, the decision you take now will be dependent upon the type of care your child has hitherto been used to.

As a parent, you have to decide what option works best for your family, for your wallet and for your child's welfare.

NURSERY
Some – but not all – nurseries operate a linked system to local primary schools.

Pros:

□ If your child has already attended this nursery, it could provide some continuity of care. It could also take the stress out of inset days and half terms because, in most circumstances, your child would simply be given the option of attending nursery all day instead (at a cost to you).

□ The friendship groups that are formed in nurseries can last through to school and could help your child make the adjustment to school more easily.

□ You know the staff and they know your child. So they are likely to pick up any changing behaviour and could alert you if, for example, your child is finding the transition to school more difficult than you envisaged. If that does happen, a nursery staffed with adults who know your child could help you tackle any such problems that arise.

Cons:

□ This is not an option that will grow with your child. Nursery facilities are really only geared to children up to the age of five. If your child is old in the school year, or particularly mature, or has an older sibling and therefore prefers to socialise with older children, this may not be an appropriate environment.

□ Some nurseries usually only provide this care option for the reception year or for infant-age children. If you choose this option, your preferred childminder or after-school club may be full by the time you want to consider a place for your child.

□ If your child is ill, they won't be able to go to nursery or school so that will mean time off work for you. You will also, most likely, still be charged for those days because they have been agreed in advance. Other options (such as nannies and childminders) might be able to look after a poorly child while you continue to work or venues such as after-school clubs and breakfast clubs might not charge you if your child cannot attend.

CHILDMINDERS

Pros:

□ Many childminders work out of one particular school, usually because they have school-age children themselves. Your child could therefore have a ready-made friendship group which might help them make the transition to a new environment.

□ Yes, childminders go on holiday but many of them work half terms, inset days and some of the longer school holidays too. Therefore you would find less interruption to your working day.

□ Childminders are all different and the care agreement you draw up will be individual to you. It is worth asking whether your childminder is prepared to have your child if, for example, they've got chickenpox and all the other children in her care have already had it.

□ If your child is ill and cannot attend, it is worth asking whether your childminder will still charge you if you keep them at home.

Cons:

□ A childminder is a more personal relationship and whilst, in nearly all circumstances, this will work beautifully, sometimes it just won't. Circumstances like this are, thankfully, very rare but they do happen.

□ Childminders are self-employed and, as such they can change their terms of business at any time. Most childminders I have met are honest, reliable, trustworthy and great communicators. However, if you're worried about a rate increase, ask if you can have a certain minimum period of notice, such as three months, so you have time to work your sums out.

□ Some childminders will ask for a down payment to keep a place open for your child. This can be as much as a month's care costs. The reason they do this is that childminders are only allowed to look after a certain number of children according to their ages, so if you have reserved a place with one childminder and you then change your mind at the last minute, you have effectively prevented that person from finding another child to fill that place. The down payment system is designed to help you make absolutely sure of your decision. If you're not sure, then don't pay and continue to look around.

HOW LONG DO YOU WANT YOUR CHILD'S DAY TO BE?

With wrap-around care, nurseries, childminders and breakfast clubs, you are effectively asking your child to cope with a day that is longer than your working day – probably by at least an hour, maybe two. Many children can cope perfectly well with that. However, some children simply don't feel they can really relax and enjoy 'down-time' unless they are at home. They might get extremely tired and extremely distressed. While many children the length and breadth of Britain will be entirely suited to an 8am–6pm day, yours may not.

SCHOOL-AFFILIATED WRAP-AROUND CARE
Pros:

□ Breakfast clubs and after-school clubs are full of your child's colleagues from school.

□ Many, though not all, are also extremely flexible.

□ At one school I know of, breakfast club doesn't have to be booked in advance. Children (and their parents if they so choose) can turn up, sign the sheet and enjoy a variety-packed breakfast for the bargain sum of £2 per person per day.

▫ Many schools aren't that flexible however and, indeed, some only have a small number of breakfast club places available. However, there is a greater emphasis on providing care before the start of the school day so facilities in this area should only improve.

▫ Breakfast clubs are also a good way of assuaging guilt. Parents are still dropping their own children off at the school gates and ensuring they have everything they need for the school day. They're simply dropping them off an hour or so before the school day starts. That gives the children greater stability and means they've still had the chance to chat on their way to school – an important part of the school day.

▫ After-school clubs are usually located near school so children can walk there.

▫ Some will even supervise homework, giving children the support they need at an appropriate time, instead of leaving children to do it with their parents much later in the evening when they're perhaps too tired to concentrate.

Cons:

▫ Some don't offer a great variety of breakfast. Some don't even have an entirely appropriate venue they can use. As with every other childcare decision, deciding whether to use breakfast clubs is all about what will work for your child and therefore for you.

▫ After-school clubs can be a ball. They can also be a bit boring. It depends on the facilities of the club, the enthusiasm of those running it and the space available to them.

▫ Some clubs might offer half-term activities but for many, when the school is shut, they are shut, so you still have to find a way to entertain your child for 13 weeks of the year on your four or five weeks of holiday.

NANNIES

You can either hire a nanny just for your child or children or, if you work part-time, you can 'job share' a nanny with another family and tailor that arrangement to suit everyone's needs.

Pros:

- Your young child doesn't have to cope with extremely long hours. They are looked after in their own home, playing with their own toys in their own space. For territorial children, those who tire easily or those who are finding the transition to school life hard, this layer of familiarity may help.
- Your nanny can still care for your child when they are sick, allowing you to continue at work. Similarly, half-terms, inset days and holidays are no problem.
- If you are delayed by a meeting and cannot get home on time, at least you know your children are being looked after safely. Do remember, however, to repay the favour by letting your nanny leave early on another day. Nannies hate nothing more than parents who take advantage and regularly leave them in the lurch.
- Whatever interests or hobbies your child has outside school can be continued, such as swimming lessons or weekly ballet/yoga/music/football.

Cons:

- Nannies cost a lot. If you are the parent of an only child it is probably not cost effective to hire a nanny. It would probably cost you as much to pay a nanny as it would to fund two children through full-time nursery.
- Some nannies will be willing to be paid only for the wrap-around hours they work during school terms and full-time hours during school holidays. Other nannies will want to be paid for the 'downtime' during the day, arguing that, by agreeing to work for you, they are unable to monetise those daytime hours.
- A good nanny can be a fantastic investment but one who is

perhaps younger or lacks the confidence to help your child with their own after-school socialising may not work for your family.

Part-time, full-time or not at all

Looking at the cost of childcare and establishing what that does to your take-home pay is just half the equation. You must also consider the costs you would incur (and the costs you would save) if you stayed at home with your child all or part of the time.

Typical savings to consider are:

- □ Commuting – if you are only going to work two or three days a week it may no longer be economical to buy a season ticket or an annual work car pass.
- □ Lunch – those who work in city centres and buy a sandwich/ soup/salad option for lunch, could be saving up to £50 a week.
- □ Miscellaneous office costs – from going out for a team drink on a Friday lunchtime to it being your turn to do the Starbucks run, there are many costs involved in just turning up to work. The office whip round for birthdays, leaving presents (and, dare I say it, maternity gifts) soon stack up. Staying at home could save £20 a week.
- □ The working wardrobe – those who work in an office or need to look smart for their job often have a wardrobe with a split personality: clothes that are suitable for work and more relaxed attire for weekends. Decent suits cost money (not to mention appropriate shoes to match). You could save £500 a year by avoiding these buys and sticking to *washable* relaxed alternatives.

Extra costs to consider

- □ Phone and fuel bills – if you're at home, you'll be using your phone (not work's) and running up your heating and lighting bills.
- □ Going out and about – If you get stir-crazy just staring at four walls with your little one, you'll want to explore playgroups and drop in centres where you can meet other parents and your

child can have a change of scene. Some are very reasonably priced (from as little as £1 a session); others cost more. **Assume £5 a week.**

□ Hobbies and ad hoc baby spending – there is an entire industry built up around entertaining children. Babies can be enrolled in swimming and music lessons from as young as six months and these can cost around £5 a session each. Then there's that gorgeous baby book you saw in Tesco as you shopped and the really cute hat you just had to get for your little one. While none of us like to think we have money to burn, it is always better to budget for at least some spending in this area than get caught out when your account dips in to overdraft at the end of the month. **Assume £10 a week.** (There is more information on babies and their day to day costs in Chapter 5.)

More than one child

□ Having more than one child can almost double the childcare bill, depending upon which option you take.

□ Second and subsequent children are usually offered a 10% discount at nurseries.

□ Childminders may have flexible policies on charging less for siblings but many don't. Always check.

□ Nannies earn a weekly wage or an annual salary (depending upon the terms you set out at the start of their contract). Having another child does not alter that price as such.

That means the cheapest option per child may not work out to be the cheapest option for your family if you have more than one child to consider.

EXTRA COSTS

For London parents sending two children to nursery full-time means finding, on average, £415 a week (or nearly £1,800 a month) on top of the mortgage and bills.

Parents across the rest of Britain will need to find an average of £335 a week (nearly £1,500 a month).

These costs have included a 10% discount for the second sibling!

At this point, when looking at the costs in black and white it is easy to feel despondent. Little wonder, then, that many parents who returned to work perfectly satisfactorily having had one child simply find it uneconomic to do so once they've had a second child. After all, not everyone in Britain is a hedge fund manager!

Whenever I've spoken to mothers about returning to work after their subsequent children, most simply give a knowing laugh. Some kept working through it all; others stopped and returned when their children were in full-time education when it made greater economic sense to so do.

That is why it is so important to ask the question:

'WHY AM I WORKING?'

To keep a career open

For those who have a highly vocational role that requires continuous professional development (such as qualified doctors or solicitors) it may seem like a struggle to keep everything going, but it is probably still better to persevere through the infant years with some kind of work/life balance if you want to keep your career going. Taking time out of such roles for prolonged periods might make it too difficult to return.

To stop you from going stir-crazy

Not all mothers feel 'stuck' at home with small children but plenty do. Returning to work – even part-time – enables them to maintain adult relationships and, most importantly, adult conversation, so not everything is all babies, babies, babies. If this is you, don't be ashamed of it. Embrace the decision: enjoy your adult environment at work and relish the precious time you set aside to be with your children.

❝ I found that putting a tight structure on the day really helped my routine and my finances. I made friends for life with the other mums I met regularly in playgroups: knowing where and when I was going helped me keep an eye on the pennies and, being an only child, Charlie could get used to mixing with other children right from the word go. ❞

Sam, mum to Charlie

Because not working is not an option

In Britain, families are predominantly either two-parent or lone parent, working families. Yes, during the infant years it can be uneconomic for one of the parents within two-parent households to keep working. For many others, they have no choice and certainly, in lone parent households, not working is simply not an option.

Cutting costs

Later on in the book (in Chapter 7), I explore ways of cutting household bills down to size to try and make life more affordable. In the meantime, let's look at ways of cutting the childcare costs down to a more manageable level.

NANNY SHARE

A nanny employed on a nanny share basis looks after the children from more than one family during her working week. There are as many ways this can work as there are examples of nannies and parents who enter into this type of arrangement. In some cases, for parents who work part-time, they literally have a nanny on the days they work and another family uses the same nanny on other days. Some nannies work with three different families each week in this way.

NANNY FACTS

61% of nannies are currently in part-time employment

15% of nannies are in a nanny share

(Source: NannyTax Annual Wages Survey 2009)

Other families have altogether different arrangements that are more akin to childminders. That is, the nanny works out of one premises but looks after the children from more than one family at that address. This can be more sociable for the children and, provided the parents, children and nanny are all happy with the arrangement, can work very well.

Each family pays their portion of the wage bill separately but the nanny still receives one pay slip with one set of take-home pay each month.

NannyTax has reported a rise in this type of arrangement as more and more families try and make ends meet. Each parent pays their portion of the nanny's National Insurance and the employer's National Insurance contributions. The nanny's wage bill can be shared on a pro rata basis according to either the number of children in her care or the number of days each family uses her services.

GRANDPARENTS

If you are lucky enough to have family living close by, you could ask whether your parents or in-laws might be prepared to have your little darling for one or two days a week. Lots of grandparents do and they can make all the difference. It could, in fact, determine whether you bring any money home from your work or whether your entire salary is swallowed up in childcare costs.

Asking family for childcare help

1. Never assume your family will want to help you on a regular basis. Many grandparents are willing and happy to help out. Many more know that the strain on their own health would make it impossible to commit to a regular arrangement. Some simply feel that they've done their bit and now it's your turn. Never assume you know the answer.

2. Think about getting to the bottom of the grandparental issue before you search for a job or return to your pre-baby job. Finding a job or agreeing terms with your existing employer and then presenting an issue almost as a *fait accompli* to your parents or in-laws may mean that they feel pressurised to help when they really don't want to. You might think that's fine but, for the arrangement to work, it needs to be stable and long-term. Why not establish what their

thoughts are on the subject first before coming up with a job and childcare plan.

3. Once you have an arrangement, make sure it is a regular commitment. Your parents, like your child, will work better with a routine. Both will know where they stand and your parents will therefore be able to plan around those arrangements accordingly.

4. Extra babysitting may be out of the question. Once any grandparents have committed to regular childminding, they may feel that they are doing enough. Asking them to babysit every Friday night as well might push the boundaries of family loyalty a little too far. So, be sensitive to their needs, no matter how much you think you are struggling.

Unless you are exceptionally lucky, grandparents will not be looking after your child or children the entire time you're at work, so you will need to consider other childcare options in addition to using their help.

Changing work

Some parents – those who take on the predominant caring role – prefer to try and change jobs to accommodate their children. Sometimes this is when they return to work after having children; other times it is when their children start pre-school or primary school.

The criteria for these parents is often that they want to be there at the school gate to drop and collect their children most days and they want to be able to provide a stable base for them during the holidays, but they don't want their brain to pickle and their family finances to go into freefall while they're doing this.

Parents of pre-school age children may choose this option to cut their working hours or their daily commute or just to be able to be there if their child is ill. Step forward the flexible working parent.

FLEXIBLE WORKING

There is a large – and growing – number of parents able to work from home. Sometimes this is as a result of a spectacular arrangement with an existing employer. Other times they have left their employment and sought more flexible working arrangements elsewhere. Some have taken the plunge and gone self-employed.

> *"As a freelance journalist I fall into the latter category. Occasionally jobs require me to make emergency childcare arrangements during a working day. Sometimes I have to book my children into holiday clubs for a week or two at a time or into breakfast clubs for a week or to beg for ad hoc help from family and friends. However, for the most part I am there at the school gate and as a taxi service for various hobbies around the place. The upside is that I don't have to remember who is minding my children and when; the downside is that I have turned jobs down that have encroached too much into that 'parent time' and therefore my earnings are limited. However, while they are of primary school age, it has been a decision that has benefited our family as a whole.*
>
> *If a job is running over, I can work on it when the kids have gone to bed and, provided I've got a good babysitter, I can attend the odd work event in the evening."*
>
> *Maddy*

Journalism is a profession that lends itself to this type of work but there are others that do so just as well. Here are examples of jobs undertaken by (predominantly) women I know who have chosen to try and fit their work around their children at home:

- Accountant
- Architect
- Builder/decorator
- Business consultant
- Caterer
- Childminder
- Dentist/dental nurse
- Facilities manager
- Family solicitor
- Gardener
- General Practice doctor (working suitable hours at a local surgery)
- Journalist
- Orthodontist
- Podiatrist/chiropodist
- Small-scale marketer
- Teacher
- Teaching assistant
- Website manager and developer
- Writer/editor

In general, these professions lend themselves more easily to flexible working than others, partly because they are generally office based and require very little in terms of specialist equipment other than the knowledge of the individual. It is relatively easy to create a little work-station in the corner of a home with a phone and a computer that can be tidied away at appropriate moments.

For those who have always been an employee, going self-employed can be a daunting step. However, the majority of parents whom I have spoken to after going down this route have felt nothing but relief after taking the plunge.

HOW TO MAKE A SUCCESS OF WORKING FROM HOME

1. **Make a business plan.** Look at what competitors charge and the service they provide for that money within your local area. Think about how much work you can realistically do in a four-hour day.
2. **Work out your family's breakeven point.** This sounds technical, but it isn't. The breakeven point is the amount of money you need to be making each week or month in order for your family to survive. Remember that you will be saving an enormous amount on childcare costs if you've previously been employed, so your breakeven point will be much lower.
3. **Prioritise cashflow.** Put money aside to fund your first three months, plus three months for cash flow issues, before you start. Whenever you get paid, immediately put your tax liability aside (25%-30% of your revenue), then save a further 15% to cover cash flow issues. Only count the remainder as your working income.

The biggest threat to small businesses (and sadly, I know this only too well) is cash flow. In 2009 alone I lost around £5,000 when jobs I had completed and invoiced for were never paid. The firms I had worked for went bust and my chances of recouping my money evaporated. That was a hefty portion of my annual income and the only thing that stopped me returning to paid employment was the money I had put aside for such emergencies. In the end, I had to survive for about four months before the next pay-cheque came in. Nasty!

More usual, for small businesses, is chasing payment from large organisations who can frequently take 90 days to come up with the money. Usually this is because of procedures such as payments only being made on one particular day each month. Whatever the reason, your very livelihood depends upon your ability to withstand the vagaries of a fluctuating cashflow.

> ❝ I set up my facilities management company three years ago when my daughter started school. Usually I don't start work for a firm until they have raised a purchase invoice for me, ensuring I'll be paid on time. I'm lucky. Not every small business person can proceed on those terms.
>
> However, after that, I've had to wait four months to get paid by one large organisation, simply because it was in the company's interests to pay me after their financial year end on 31 December. ❞
>
> Jacky, facilities manager

These things happen to small businesses all the time. The only way to survive is to realise this, account for it, not get unduly angered by it, and to chase outstanding invoices promptly and politely but firmly. For more advice contact the Professional Contractors' Group (PCG) at **www.pcg.org.uk**. It is the professional association for freelancers, contractors and consultants and they have a wealth of information and third party professional contacts such as CreditSafe Ltd (**www.creditsafe.co.uk**), a firm that specialises in chasing outstanding debts for clients.

Cutting household bills down to size

The first thing to consider when assessing what working and childcare arrangements you can afford is whether your money is working as efficiently as it can.

Before your baby is born you have the time to look through every element of your finances to see if your money is working as hard as possible for you. All of these elements are detailed in Chapter 7. They explain what to look at, when and which items to examine together to maximise your savings.

However, given that this is a vital part of working out whether you can afford to return to work and finance childcare, here is a little look at what cost savings a typical family could make.

- Just by shopping sensibly the average family can save as much as £150 a month on food and provisions.
- Cutting out just one takeaway a week could save £100 a month.
- Standard variable mortgage rates have risen recently and look set to do so again as lenders anticipate base rate rises. Dig out your mortgage documents and check you are not overpaying. On an average £150,000 mortgage you could save approximately £100 a month for every 1% less in interest that you pay.
- Look at getting an online utilities deal. Many providers charge less for a dual fuel online tariff than other kinds. You could save £200 a year (nearly £20 a month) or more by switching. What's more, paying by direct debit usually works out cheaper than paying quarterly.
- Combining television, broadband and telephone bills could save even more.

Based on these estimates, the average family could save nearly £400 a month – enough to cover half the average monthly cost for a full-time childminder place. Some of these savings are conservative estimates. Information on how to accomplish such savings is detailed in Chapter 7.

4. Planning for your family should the worst happen

Having a baby is great. It comes with a tumult of emotions, sleepless nights, a realisation of your role as simply a conduit of knowledge for the next generation: you name it, you can experience it.

However, parenthood also brings a whole raft of responsibility. As providers and carers for the next generation every parent bears responsibility for considering the practical elements of life – even if that means getting to grips with the unthinkable: not being there to see your children grow up.

Making a will

It is all too easy to get wrapped up in everyday things and ignore this most pressing problem. None of us wants to think about not being there to see our children grow up but, if the worst did happen, having no plans in place would make an already tragic situation almost unbearable. As parents, whether married, joined in a civil union, or just co-habiting, making a will is absolutely vital.

Research from Consumer Focus (formally the National Consumer Council [NCC]) suggests there are more than 27 million adults in England and Wales who have failed to make a will. For those who are not in a long-term relationship or have no children, there's probably little need. However, sadly, many of those who do need a will (for example, parents of young children) are the least likely to have one.

You have just had the single biggest reason to make a will: a dependent child.

When people die who haven't made a will their estate goes 'intestate' – that means it is up to lawyers to decide how best to distribute the assets and try and guess what that person would have intended to do. There are laws in place to help this process but even the best legal minds using a fair system cannot hope to get it right all of the time.

Those who haven't made a will are running the risk that:
- Their estate could go to the wrong people
- The tax man could take too big a share
- There could be legal claims made on the estate by disgruntled family members
- Their children are not cared for by the person they would have chosen

Reasons to make a will:
- To decide who inherits and how much
- To avoid Inheritance Tax as far as possible (the current threshold is £325,000)
- To appoint legal guardians for your children
- To set up trusts for your children should you die before they reach adulthood
- To choose trustees to help manage those trusts for your children
- To appoint executors (who can also be the trustees should you wish)

This is particularly important for the estimated two million co-habiting couples in Britain today and those who have multiple families due to divorce and subsequent new relationships.

Despite moves by both the government and the legal profession to change the status quo, co-habiting couples can still be treated very differently in law from married couples or same sex couples who have entered a civil partnership.

For example, unmarried couples still have no automatic right to leave money or assets to each other free from Inheritance Tax and, without a will, those partners might not automatically inherit anything.

What's more, those who have been married, have since divorced and moved on to a new unmarried partnership, may find their former spouse has a greater claim on their assets than their current partner. The waters are muddied even further when children are thrown into the mix.

The Law Commission is looking at whether UK law should be amended but, until it is, the onus is on all parents and cohabiting couples to make sure they have a good, clear, up-to-date will in place.

> ❝ The rules for people who are married can be fairly straight-forward and largely common sense. However, the rules are definitely *not the same* for people who live together as *common law husband and wife.* Wills can be changed. Making one is not expensive. There are will-writers who will visit you, if you cannot face a visit to your solicitor. ❞
>
> George Emsden, independent financial adviser for
> www.georgeemsden.co.uk

THE THREE WAYS TO MAKE A WILL
The DIY option
WH Smith and other major newsagents sell DIY will packs for around £20. They include explanatory notes and should be easy to follow. However, DIY kits don't enable you to get advice about whether your will is appropriate or check that you've factored everything in.

Will-writing services
There are many online will-writing services that cost a little more (about £30) but also include a free legal check. They can be found easily through any search engine. There are many good services out there, however

many of the staff within these companies are **not** solicitors and the will-writing industry itself is not regulated. Unless you go via a personal recommendation or a professional contact from, say, your financial adviser (if you have one) you have little way of knowing anything about the quality of service you are receiving. The Law Society is lobbying the government to regulate the will-writing industry, having compiled a dossier of case studies involving problems with unregulated will-writers.

The advice route

DIY is all very well but are you up to speed with Inheritance Tax rules? How are you going to protect your hard earned assets from the tax office and make sure your loved ones or your favourite charities benefit as you intended? This is what solicitors are for and what they do best. DIY services make sure your will is valid but they will not advise you on the most appropriate way to shield your assets from the taxman, nor will they ensure you have considered most options available to you. A good solicitor can cost upwards of £200 + VAT for a comprehensive will service. However, for complete peace of mind and knowledge that every eventuality has been considered this can be a price worth paying.

You can search on the Law Society's own website for an appropriate solicitor near to your home/work at **www.lawsociety.org.uk**.

THINGS TO PREPARE

Firstly, you'll need to bring some documents with you to prove who you are and where you live. A recent bill and a passport usually suffice.

Then you'll need to think about some of the issues you'll have to address.

- □ **Your executor/trustee**. This can be your partner/spouse but it is also helpful to have a second name (perhaps the solicitor) who can take decisions should circumstances change and your partner is no longer able to act.
- □ **Suitable guardians**. Try and decide who you would wish to raise your children as legal guardians should both you and your partner die. Gruesome though this process is, it's considerably better than the alternative – letting others try and make those decisions for you.

□ **Legacies.** Are there any particular gifts of money, jewellery or other specific items you wish to leave to named individuals or charities? Compiling a list now will save time (and possibly money, as solicitors work on an hourly fee basis).

WHERE TO GO FOR MORE ADVICE

Wills & Probate is a book penned by Which? that gives advice on how to make a will and how to administer an estate, with or without employing a solicitor. The book also deals with how to administer the estate of someone who has died (probate). It is available at bookshops priced £10.99, or can be ordered via the Which? website at www.which.co.uk.

FINDING A GOOD LAWYER

The Law Society (www.lawsociety.org.uk/home.law) has a section where you can search for a specialist solicitor by postcode. By using the dropdown menu, selecting 'wills & probate' and typing in the postcode where you live or work, you can find a selection of good solicitors in your area.

UNTANGLING LEGAL PROBLEMS

Citizens Advice Bureaux rely upon thousands of qualified individuals volunteering their time to give advice to people who really need it. Many solicitors volunteer to help in their local bureau and, if you have a problem you need to address, they can be a fantastic first port of call. If nothing else, they can usually recommend where you should go for more help. (www.citizensadvice.org.uk).

Beyond your will

COMPANY BENEFITS

Ensuring your assets are properly distributed in the event of your death does not begin and end with a will. For example, many people have 'death in service' benefits with their employers that can be assigned however they choose. They can also be updated with a simple **letter of wish**. Your HR department should know whether you can assign your benefit with an **expression of wish** form or with a simple letter stating your wishes.

PENSION SCHEMES

Similarly, many private and company pension schemes have a widow's pension benefit which can be assigned to anyone you choose in the event of your death. If you are unsure, look at your pension policy. There, you should find both a policy number for your particular scheme and a telephone number for general enquiries. If you want to know who gets what in the event of your death, just ask. Again, it is important to make sure any plans in place suit your family's circumstances. If they don't, change how it is assigned with an expression of wish form or letter.

Paying the bills when things go wrong

If you do nothing to safeguard yourself against worst-case scenarios, you might not be in a position to help your children fulfil their dreams and ambitions as they grow up. You might not even be in a position to afford to put food on the table or keep a roof over your head.

Basically, if a key earner in your household dies, or becomes too ill to work, or loses their job and cannot find another one easily, how do you keep paying the bills?

> ❝ Nearly one child in 20 loses a parent before they've finished full time education. ❞
>
> Martin Lewis, Moneysaving Expert

There are a variety of insurances out there that all aim to provide cash to cover such unforeseen events. Some will pay out in more circumstances than others. Some cost considerably more. Some will only cover illness; others only pay out if you die. Others pay out if you lose your job (under certain circumstances). Basically, you get what you pay for, but here is a brief guide to what the options are (and what they cost).

LEVEL TERM ASSURANCE

This is life insurance. It pays out a fixed lump sum if you die during the term of the product. You choose how long you want cover for and how much money you want to be paid in the event of your death. It is one of the most cost effective types of insurance around and, because it will only pay out for one type of event (ie your death) it is relatively easy to compare different products and get the best value deal.

Do I need it?
If you cannot think how those around you will pay the bills and keep a roof over their heads when you're gone, the answer is an unequivocal 'yes'.

How long should I insure myself for?
To be sensible, a policy should last until your children reach adulthood or until they finish full-time education, whichever is later.

How much will it cost?
As with any insurance product, the younger you are and the fitter you are perceived to be, the less it will cost. If you smoke or work in a dangerous occupation (the armed services, police, scaffolding, mining, or sky diving for example) you will pay more. If you are a 20-year-old aerobics instructor who doesn't smoke or drink, you'll probably pay very little.

How much cover do I need?
1. Take the amount of your outstanding mortgage.
2. Then take the amount you need to cover all other living expenses each month and multiply this by 12 to get an annual amount.
3. Try and multiply that annual sum up to take account of the number of years you face before your kids either leave full-time education or reach adulthood. So if your youngest child is five now and you wish to insure yourself until they're 21, multiply your costs by 16.
4. Now add on some extra expenses such as the cost of childcare and the cost of your funeral.

The Consumers' Association, Which? says that when you first calculate what cover you could need, you're likely to be in for a shock.

CALCULATING WHAT COVER YOU NEED

If you calculate your family might need £3,000 to cover them for immediate needs and £1,000 a month for 20 years, the total amount of cover needed would be £243,000 (£1,000 x 12 x 20, plus £3000). And this is just for family protection. You still need to make sure you have life cover in place to pay off your mortgage if you die.

Source: Which?

If you can't afford to pay for this level of cover, don't panic. The main thing is not to overstretch yourself. Just be realistic and insure yourself for as near to your target figure as is feasible. It's better to have some life cover in place than none.

If you are a full-time carer

Don't assume that, just because you don't bring an income home, your family wouldn't be financially any worse off without you. They would. So, you should factor in appropriate childcare costs. There is more detail on this in Chapter 3, but briefly, NannyTax estimates the average take home pay for a full-time nanny is between £258 and £328 a week. That figure is net of tax and excludes employers' National Insurance contributions. Basically, it would gross up to about £20,000–£26,000 a year. Clearly, as children grow, you wouldn't need to factor this kind of financial support into your figures for the next 20 years, but it is realistic to assume your family could do with this kind of support for at least five years (depending on the age of your kids).

Where to go for best value

Where better to go for a word of advice on the subject than those canny researchers from Which? They always research life and protection policies and come up with some Best Buys, taking the legwork out of the process for anyone who feels bamboozled by choice.

Here they show what the lowest monthly premiums were in December 2009 for level term policies paying £100,000 of cover.

20 year term	Company	Monthly premium
Male non smoker age 44	AA insurance services	£14.20
Female non smoker age 44	Barclays Life	£11.41
25 year term		
Male non smoker age 39	AA Insurance Services	£10.87
Female non smoker age 39	Barclays Life	£8.81
30 year term		
Male non smoker age 34	AA Insurance Services	£8.90
Female non smoker age 34	AA Insurance Services	£7.10

(Source: Which?)

I have only shown non smokers. Smokers will get charged considerably more (usually between 50% and 100% more). For example, a male smoker, aged 34, could expect to pay £10.83 a month with Barclays Life; a female smoker of the same age would pay £8.54 a month, also with Barclays Life.

Comparing costs

There are some good comparison sites around that would be able to give you an idea of how much you could pay. The websites **www.moneyfacts. co.uk** and **www.moneysupermarket.com** both have a good selection of insurance providers you could question.

PROTECTING YOUR FAMILY IF YOU CANNOT WORK

Contemplating and planning for life's worst case scenarios is scary enough. It does not need to be made worse by the impenetrable fog of jargon and exclusions that so many insurance companies use. Sadly, insurance companies insist on being about as user-friendly as a chocolate teapot in this department. So, you need to know what you want and how it works before you even start to look to compare products and prices.

A rough guide to cover

Basically, there's little point in being insured up to the hilt in case you die and ignore the fact that what scuppers most families is one or other parent falling ill and being unable to work, and therefore unable to meet the bills.

There are a number of policies that can pay out if you are unable to work for a variety of reasons:

- **Income Protection (or Permanent Health Insurance)**. This pays a monthly sum of tax-free income in case you cannot work through illness or disability. It pays up to a maximum of 65% of your earnings, depending on the policy. It is designed to carry on once any employer's benefits cease and is also suitable for the self-employed. Multiple claims can be made on one policy, provided it is still paid up.

- **Critical Illness Cover**. This pays a lump sum if you are diagnosed with a serious illness. Such a sum could be used to pay for modifications to the home, to pay any outstanding mortgage or to hire childcare while you undergo treatment and recovery. Policies can be combined with life policies although they will only pay out once.

- **Accident, Sickness and Unemployment (ASU) cover**. These policies can cover unemployment, sickness and accidents, or all three eventualities. ASU cover usually pays an income for one or two years and is designed to bridge the gap between earning periods due to these prescribed events. ASU policies only allow the holder to claim once.

CASE STUDY

Jeanette was a go-getting mum with an eight-year-old daughter when she was diagnosed with breast cancer back in 2006. It was a Grade 4 cancer that was already in her lymph glands and Jeanette immediately underwent a full mastectomy and had aggressive treatment (luckily her healthcare trust paid for Herceptin).

Her life was soon taken up with a year-long session of treatment that included gruelling rounds of chemotherapy, radiotherapy and Herceptin (administered intravenously), after which she endured two breast reconstructions.

'I've always had savings and I've always had a good salary. You never think for a moment that you'll be so ill that even after a year, you'll still need help.'

Jeanette's savings lasted her a year. She was also lucky enough to have an insurance policy through her work that paid 50% of her salary after the first three months. She is still surviving on that.

So, for the first year, Jeanette and her husband managed to keep everything going through a combination of the insurance policy and her savings. After that, the savings ran out.

Jeanette was lucky. She went to see her mortgage company, Nationwide, who enabled her to take a payment holiday on her mortgage while she was recovering. When she does start earning again, Jeanette will of course have a much bigger debt, but at least she has kept a roof over her head.

'I still feel very lucky. I've got no savings, the credit cards are maxed out and I've a massive overdraft etc, but I'm very, very lucky. I have a friend who had the same cancer. She lost her job because her firm just couldn't keep her on. She ended up losing her home and is now living in a static caravan.'

Jeanette planned, she had savings, she had insurance and still she couldn't keep all her financial commitments going. Thankfully now she's been given the all clear and is looking to return to work.

What's good about these policies?

If you have a serious illness, such as cancer, and have to endure invasive surgery or radical treatment such as chemotherapy and radiotherapy, the last thing you need to worry about is trying to keep hold of a job to pay the bills. Policies like this are designed to ensure you can keep a roof over your family's head during such times.

What's bad about them?

The insurance company (that profit-making colossus owned by shareholding pension funds) is the one that determines whether your illness is serious. It is not enough to know you have cancer. You must have been diagnosed with one of the particular cancers as laid out in the small print of your policy's terms and conditions. That is why the Consumers' Association prefers to recommend Income Protection as the greater catch-all type of insurance policy. You can either take out insurance that covers 'any occupation' – which will only pay out if you become too ill to work in any occupation – or you can take an 'own occupation' – a policy that will pay out if you become too ill to carry on in your own line of work. Such policies can cover mental as well as physical illnesses.

WHERE TO GO FOR MORE ADVICE

The best thing to do, if you are interested in taking out some sort of protection policy, is to get good, solid, independent financial advice. You can start your search for a local Independent Financial Advisor (IFA) who specialises in insurance and protection on Unbiased (www.unbiased.co.uk), the website established to help you find local, professional advice.

HOW MUCH THE ADVICE WILL COST

Different IFAs work in different ways. Some charge a fee, which can be as much as £250 an hour. Others don't charge you directly but they get paid commission by the provider of the policy you take out. If you don't take out a policy, they don't get paid. Whichever way your chosen IFA works, they are obliged to tell you BEFORE you start the advice process and check you're happy to proceed on this basis.

ONLINE HELP

Not everyone wants to go down the IFA route, but some people still want to know more before they take the plunge. Two places to go for a little more information online are:

- www.moneysavingexpert.com. Here Martin Lewis gives a more detailed explanation of the detailed types of cover available and what you might expect to pay.

- www.which.co.uk. Which? regularly produces a comprehensive guide to protection and insurance policies. To save you a little legwork, some of their data has been reproduced in this book.

What to do if you don't have cover

At the end of the day it costs your mortgage company time and money in dealing with you if you fall behind with your payments because of illness so contact them. Some are flexible; others aren't.

Remember:

- ☐ Talk to your lender
- ☐ If they are not being helpful, go and get advice; **www.citizensadvice.org.uk** is a great first port of call

What not to do

Don't be tempted to accept the services of a company that will only promise to help you for a fee. They don't have your best interests at heart. Make sure you go somewhere that's reputable and free.

Savings

Children are expensive and noisy and can strip you of every resource (time, money, energy, emotional resilience) you have and more. However, they also focus the mind. Many a parent looks upon the arrival of their child or children as an opportunity to assess what kind of future they hope their offspring can achieve. What kind of school or university career can they envisage for their children? What kind of adults will they become? What job path will they want to take? Can we, as parents, help them to realise those dreams?

CHILD TRUST FUNDS

When Gordon Brown was still Chancellor, Child Trust Funds were launched as a way of enabling parents to build a nest egg for their children – some money to help them enter adult life, if you will.

These accounts work a bit like ISAs (Individual Savings Accounts) in that a certain amount can be invested each year and it will earn interest, tax free. In the case of CTFs, that annual limit is set at £1200.

To kick start the process, the government will give parents a voucher worth £250 to invest in a Child Trust Fund of their choice. This is to start the savings ball rolling. At the moment, children also receive a further £250 investment in their Child Trust Fund when they reach age 7. [N.B. This may change after the 2010 election.] CTFs were launched in April 2005 (and backdated to 1 September 2002) and the first children eligible to receive their top up turned seven on 1 September 2009.

Types of Child Trust Funds

There are two types of CTFs: cash and equity.

□ **Cash CTFs** work just like regular savings accounts. You put money in, you keep it stashed away and, at the end of the term you get your money back plus accumulated interest.

The amount you invest is never at risk, but then again, your earnings potential is limited.

□ **Equity CTFs** are stock market-backed savings vehicles. The money you invest is used to buy shares and is managed by a fund manager. Because the fund manager has to make decisions about your investment (which shares to buy, which to sell and which to hold) there will be annual management charges on the account (limited to 1.5% of the value of the investment). These are the types of CTFs recommended by the government because, over the nearly 18 years that the investment will run, they are almost certain to outperform cash savings. However, there is a risk with this type of investment. If there is another stock market crash, for example, share prices might plummet and the investment you have made for your child's future may therefore not grow as much as you anticipated. There is also the (extremely) slight possibility that you don't get back as much as you have invested over the period. Those risks are extremely small – especially over such a long period of time – but they cannot be discounted entirely.

What's good about CTFs?

CTFs are brilliant for two main reasons:

□ The government is giving you money to invest for your child. Even if you put nothing else aside in a CTF, you get £250 to invest in the first year of your child's life and £250 when they turn seven. Nationwide Building Society estimated that, in the case of children born on 1st January 2010, this £500 would grow to around £850 by the time that child turns 18.

□ While that's not going to set the world on fire, it is assuming that rates remain ridiculously low (at 0.5%) for the whole period, so this could be more. At today's prices, it would be enough to pay for the deposit on a flat rental or a term's university accommodation.

WHAT REGULAR SAVING CAN ACHIEVE

Nationwide Building Society has looked at what a child, born on 1 January 2010, could have saved by the time he or she reaches age 18 using a cash CTF.

- Scenario 1: putting nothing aside. The government's £500 contribution could grow to £856 by age 18.
- Scenario 2: saving £20 a month (£240 a year). Approximately £4,320 of parental savings plus £500 of government money would grow to £5,921 by 18.
- Scenario 3: saving the full £1,200 a year. Putting £1,200 a year aside means saving around £21,600. That, plus the government's £500 could grow to a sizeable nest egg of £25,894.

All these figures are based on current interest rates, which are at historic lows.

Putting this into perspective: the Push student debt survey. Students who started their studies in autumn 2009 can expect to graduate with debts of £23,500. So, at today's rates:

- Parents putting £20 a month aside could help their child avoid debt for most of their first year of university.
- Those fully funding a CTF could help their child to graduate, debt free, from university.

That means, by the time your children reach university age, your child's fully funded CTF should still fund half of a standard degree course.

What's bad about CTFs?

Child Trust Funds are the property of the child. Once that money has been locked away, the only person that can access it is the child when he or she turns 18. Some parents may reasonably worry that their child might not be financially responsible enough to deal with a bunch of cash on their 18th birthday. The nightmare scenario, for example, could be that parents have squirrelled away £1,200 a year only to watch their precious offspring blow the lot on a spectacular gap year of partying.

As with Individual Savings Accounts, there is a limit to how much can be invested in CTFs. Those who want to put more aside will have to do so elsewhere (see 'what are the alternatives?' below).

WATCH THIS SPACE

The British government is mired in record levels of debt and all political parties are trying to find ways to cut that debt down to size. Child Trust Funds may not continue in their current form.

WHAT ARE THE ALTERNATIVES?

Child Trust Funds may offer a tax-free way to save but they are not the only savings option available. One of my children is too old to qualify for Child Trust Funds (by 13 months!) so I have had to research alternative savings options. Of course all of these can be used in addition to the CTF, rather than instead of one. Parents who worry about handing their children a big lump of cash at 18 might prefer to retain a CTF just for the government's contribution and invest their own money somewhere they retain control for longer.

HIGH STREET SAVINGS ACCOUNTS

The point of a children's savings account is not just somewhere to earn top interest: it is a place where your children can go with you and get into the habit of putting money aside; where they can watch that money grow and where they can develop a savings habit that could stand them in good stead as adults.

SPEND HALF, SAVE HALF

Whether it is gifts from grandparents, godparents, friends or family, your children will receive money for birthdays and/or Christmas. Teaching them what to do with that money is a lesson they will remember. (See Chapter 11 for more on pocket money.) The old mantra of spend half, save half is one that many parents still use (me included).

My daughter was lucky enough to win £50 on the premium bonds. I took her straight down to the building society and we paid the cheque into her account and drew half out. She really enjoyed spending that money (on a cinema trip for the family). She had a fantastic day and the memory of that day is something we still talk about. That memory could not have been bettered had she spent twice as much.

It's important to remember that children's savings accounts are not automatically tax-free. Each child is treated just like an adult in the eyes of the tax office, with a personal allowance, so children can earn up to £6,475 on salary, savings or investment income before they are taxed. However, there is one important extra rule to remember: money deposited by parents is only tax-free on returns (that is, interest earned) of up to £100 per parent.

That said, a regular high-street savings vehicle is important for financial education, for flexible savings, and for allowing your children to learn when to put money aside and what things are suitable items to be paid for out of savings.

At the time of writing, with Bank of England base rates so laughably low, many high street names are paying derisory amounts of interest on kids' savings. Accounts offered by Royal Bank of Scotland, Lloyds, Abbey, Barclays, Britannia, Northern Rock, Co-op, and many more pay rates of 0.5% or less. Some, such as Yorkshire Bank and Newcastle Building Society are paying just 0.1% in interest.

Finding a suitable account is easy if you look on websites such as **www.moneysupermarket.com** or **www.moneyfacts.co.uk**. I found rates between 5% and 2% offered by a variety of reputable building societies. But first, read Martin Lewis's words of wisdom on **www.moneysavingexpert.com**.

He and his team update the site regularly and find ways to exploit any bank loopholes that can maximise the return on your money.

REGULAR SAVINGS

Think about how you save for your child. It could be that you put some of the Child Benefit away into an account each month that can quite easily be locked away. Meanwhile, your child puts birthday and Christmas money aside and perhaps some pocket money, knowing that it can be accessed regularly to buy things for family and friends or longed-for items on an ad hoc basis. If that's the case, why not open an instant access account for your child to see, touch and use, to learn about savings while you earn more interest using a regular savings account in their name.

Whereas the best instant access account paid around 2% when I researched them, the best regular savings account paid 5% and the nearest rival 4% (from the Principality and Scottish Building Societies respectively). It therefore makes sense to invest between £10 and £150 a month in something like this for a year to maximise the interest payable. At the end of the year, the money is usually transferred to an instant access account paying a much lower rate of interest. At that time, you can decide where you'd like that money to go.

SAVINGS BEHAVIOUR

Here's how to build up a pattern of savings behaviour that could earn your kids a fortune in interest and generate a pattern of behaviour that will teach them how to assess value.

1. Have an instant access savings account which your child uses to put money aside regularly.
2. At the same time, open a regular savings account and put some of your Child Benefit aside on your child's behalf each month.
3. At the end of the year, your regular savings will revert to an instant access account. At this point, review all savings options in the marketplace for this money AND for your child's existing instant access account.
4. Transfer everything to the best player in the marketplace.

5. Start another regular savings account for another 12 months with the market leading interest rate.
6. Repeat each year.

Just make sure you pay close attention to how much interest your child's money is earning. Before long, you might want to be looking at tax-free options. Once a year should be enough for this.

MONEY SAVING EXPERT SHOWS YOU HOW MUCH INTEREST RATES MATTER

Save £1,500 in a poor-paying children's account over three years and you'd earn £5 interest, but by picking the best you could boost the returns to £100. This is £89 more for kids of a higher rate taxpayer than the top paying adult instant access savings account.

	Rate	Interest Earnt	Extra Interest (5)
Poor Adult Account (1)	0.1%	£4 basic rate tax £3 higher rate taxpayer	N/A
Poor Children's Account (2)	0.1%	£5	£2
Top Adults' Account (3)	3.30%	£123 basic rate taxpayer £92 higher rate taxpayer	£120 £89
Top Children's Account (4)	2.20%	£101	£98

Please note rates for this chart were sourced when base rates were 0.5%.

TAX-FREE SAVINGS FOR KIDS

Child Trust Funds are not the only places where your children's savings can earn money tax free. National Savings and Investments (NS&I – the premium bond people) also offers a tax-free savings vehicle. It's called Children's Bonus Bonds.

How they work

Parents can invest multiples of £25 up to a maximum per bond of £3,000 which is then locked away for five years. The interest it earns is tax free. At the moment, Bonus Bonds are paying 2.5% AER tax free which means that, if you invest £1,000 you will have £1,131.41 after five years.

On maturity, that money can either be withdrawn, or, if parents are putting money aside now to help with their child's university education or other costs they may face in adulthood, these can be rolled over five years at a time.

The good news for parents (like me who worry about handing over a big pile of cash from a Child Trust Fund, for example, on their child's 18th birthday), is that the money remains under parental control until that parent deems their child is responsible enough. That could be when their child reaches age 25 if they think it's more appropriate.

The bad news is that the interest is fixed for five years at a time. If interest rates or inflation change significantly during that time, Children's Bonus Bonds may not have earned nearly as much in interest as rival products.

SAVE NOW FOR BIG BILLS LATER

However you choose to put money aside for your child, one thing is certain: it is better to do that while they are small. Children become more, not less, expensive as they grow up.

University

The costs of attending university are increasing by around £4,000 a year and university students who started their courses in October 2009 can expect to graduate with an average of £23,500 in debt; more if they have chosen a London university. Fully funding a Child Trust Fund could cover the cost of a child's university years. Estimates of the returns on equity Child Trust Funds are significantly greater than the calculated returns of cash CTFs. Projections suggest that fully funded equity CTFs could yield around £30,000 or more compared to £23,500 for a fully funded cash CTF.

School fees

For those wanting to fund private education, a Child Trust Fund won't come close.

To put things into perspective, putting the maximum away into a cash ISA from the moment your child is born until the time they reach secondary school would mean investing nearly £40,000. Given that secondary school places cost around £13,000 each year (more if you live in London), then putting £300 a month aside from birth would just about give you enough to fund half their secondary education.

That is the sort of commitment that requires significant financial advice and a significant commitment from you from birth.

Hobbies

Some hobbies are free; some cost a great deal. The older your child gets, the more expensive a hobby becomes because the better your child becomes.

Take learning an instrument as an example.

Many schools teach children in shared lessons to begin with and parents can usually rent instruments until they know whether or not their child is going to take to their new hobby. That can mean lessons cost £80 a term and instruments cost a further £30–£50 a term to hire. Buying a used instrument off eBay is a good bet, given that you could sell it on again afterwards. Of course, once your child becomes good, that means individual lessons (costing £15–£30 for half an hour depending on their standard and your location) and instruments become more expensive. Learning a stringed instrument, such as a violin, means buying a new one each time your child grows until they reach 'full-size' around the age of 14.

It's not just music that costs. One parent despaired when her daughter – a good swimmer – left her custom-made swimsuit in the pool after a 6am training session. These suits (the sort that Rebecca Adlington wears) cost around £200 each. Lessons can cost upwards of £100 a term and then there's the cost of travelling to competitions around the country (and overseas).

Hobbies are great. They give your children broader skills they can carry with them right through to adulthood and beyond and they provide an alternative means of socialising well into adulthood. They teach them the benefit of practice, of competition, of acquiring a skill. Sporting hobbies lead to a physical wellbeing that can combat sedentary lifestyles and obesity and can set children's metabolism and dietary habits up for life. Just don't be fooled into thinking that the seven-a-side football team your son joins age six is going to be cheap. It might cost £70 a term for soccer coaching; £50 a term in team subs and pitch hire; and a further £40 in kit. That's a nice £400 a year.

There are plenty of ways of cutting those hobby costs down to size on page 120. In the meantime, while your child is relatively cheap, it is worth gaining an understanding of how quickly and how rapidly the costs of raising your little darling can escalate.

> ❝ A friend once said to me people love to give to babies, not so much to small children, and by the time you need money for trainers, no one is interested. On this note, save all money given to small children and babies and use it when they need trainers/computer games etc. ❞
>
> Claire, mum to Jack and Hamish

5. The first year

Congratulations. You have a big bundle of joy, demanding time, energy and money – and you probably haven't slept properly since you (or your partner) were seven months pregnant. Your once stylish capsule wardrobe now has tell-tale stains on the shoulder of every outfit and black is no longer a practical colour to wear. Welcome to parenthood.

Preparing for your child's arrival was one thing. Adapting to your baby's changing needs while keeping everything manageable is quite another.

Getting the everyday stuff right

At this age, your baby has very simple needs: eat, sleep, excrete. Making sure you and your partner can deal with this day-to-day routine easily and cheaply, both at home and on the go, is all that's important right now.

Luckily all of your child's financial needs at this age can be accommodated within the Child Benefit allowance, which is payable to the nominated parent of every child under the age of 17. Current levels are £20.30 per week for a parent's first child and £13.40 per week for each subsequent child. This is usually paid four-weekly but can be paid weekly under certain circumstances. (There's more information about Child Benefit in Chapter 2.)

However, that is all the Child Benefit covers, so those who have savings may be safe for now but might feel the pinch later.

EATING

Milk: the elixir of life. Health visitors and antenatal class facilitators have probably already talked at length about the breast vs bottle debate. This book isn't here to extol the virtues of one over the other. I know mothers who always hated breastfeeding but ended up breastfeeding for more than a year. I know others who desperately wanted to breastfeed and simply couldn't. Either their babies wouldn't latch on or they just could not produce enough milk to keep their children satisfied. Having fallen into the latter category myself and resorted to bottle feeding after a painful and frustrating three months with each of my children, I'm certainly the last person who can pass comment on this issue.

However, there is no escaping the economics of the situation.

Breast milk	Formula milk
Breast milk is free	Formula milk costs money. The cheapest I could find (using **www.mysupermarket.co.uk**) cost £7.25 for a jar that would last a week.
It is already sterile	You'd need to sterilise bottles, costing from £10 for a steriliser (see Chapter 1)
It comes in its own replenish-able container	Bottles and teats also cost money. £9 for six teats that would last around two months. That works out at £1.25 a week
You may need to express milk for others to feed your child. That means borrowing or investing in a breast pump (£15) and spending the same money on bottles and teats as a bottle fed baby.	There are no incremental costs to going out and about or returning to work. You already have the kit and have budgeted for it.

Breast Milk Total: £15 for a pump, £10 for a steriliser, £10 a month for teats, £10 a month for formula (because you probably won't be able to be there constantly to breastfeed or express enough to exclusively use breast milk). **That's £45 set-up costs plus £20 thereafter.**

Formula Milk total: £10 secondhand steriliser, £10 a month for teats, £30 a month for formula. **That's £50 set-up costs plus £40 a month thereafter.**

Does your newborn need special formula?

Formula is expensive and if your little one suffers from bad reactions to standard cow's milk-based formula, talk to your health visitor and/or your doctor.

My daughter suffered from terrible eczema, which was exacerbated by formula. I eventually found a formula that suited her. Sadly, it cost an eye-watering £15 a week, leaving me substantially out of pocket. However, an unrelated meeting with my local GP a few months later led to an interesting revelation: some baby milk formula is available on prescription, and often for reasonably minor conditions.

Different conditions may be exacerbated by milk based products in different ways. Lactose intolerance, reflux and breathing problems are just three of the more common side effects. Health professionals have a huge long list of different formulas that they are able to offer on prescription for babies that have recognised symptoms. And because prescriptions are free, that means parents of poorly children often don't have to break the bank to ensure they can raise a healthy baby.

Can your feeding patterns fit round your return to work?

For mothers who do plan to continue breastfeeding, there are logistics to consider when returning to work. The main concern is likely to be whether it is possible to express milk during the day.

For this you will need:

- A breast pump
- Sterile bottles
- Secure screw top lids
- Somewhere appropriate (a fridge or insulated coolbag) to store expressed milk

That is all quite simple to arrange. The more difficult logistical issue is finding somewhere discreet to express away. The girls' loos are not really the best answer. In many cases, there may be another solution.

Years ago when I worked for a bank, a colleague of mine arranged to have a chair and a fridge put in the stationery cupboard, along with a lock on the inside of the door. That way, she could express milk somewhere discreet, without being disturbed. Of course, not every work venue will have somewhere appropriate. Some parents who had hoped to feed their baby exclusively with breast milk might find they have to compromise with a half-and-half approach and expand their monthly budget to include supplemental formula.

SLEEPING

For the first three months of your child's life, when they are not asleep in the cot or Moses basket, they are probably having a nap in the car seat or pushchair. Infant car seats are truly fantastic for giving new parents the utmost portability. You can visit anyone knowing that when your child is tired, they can have a short kip in a comfy, familiar place.

However, that doesn't last long. Babies grow all too quickly and what once felt like a comfortable – and safe – place for a short daytime nap will soon feel restrictive. Time to buy a travel cot.

Travel cots are marvellous; they take just seconds to assemble or disassemble and they can last children a good couple of years. They're great for visiting friends, relatives, for weekends away or just to keep in case of emergency (or if the antenatal friends come round and one of their babies needs a sleep). What's more, they are another great item to purchase secondhand.

TOP DEAL

I searched for the best price for a Graco Compact Primary travel cot

- RRP £55 from mothercare.com, now retailing at £44 and saving £11
- RRP £45 from babythings4U, now on offer for £36 and saving £9
- eBay was £16 plus £10.50 p&p, costing £26.50 and saving £9.50 on the cheapest available elsewhere online

Lowest to highest price difference: £28.50

Best spots

- School newsletter: travel cot cost just £10
- Freecycle: two travel cots in the last two months in my local area cost £0

Beware of false economies

Ideally, every family should need no more than one travel cot that will be sturdy and serve all their children admirably before it is then passed on to friends or relatives, or sold. Our travel cot did just that. It was a Little Tikes model and served both my children until they were at least two years old, as well as my cousin's little girl, and is still as good as new.

They retail for around £35 new or £10 on eBay or in charity shops or church notice boards.

Compare and contrast this to the reasonably new product that is the Samsonite pop-up travel cot. Parenting magazines and the NCT have really taken this product to heart. I can see why. It is gorgeous to look at, it provides a great little bed for a baby on the go and it is easy to assemble and lightweight. What's more, it retails at around £28–£35. So it costs no more than my travel cot.

However, children can only use it until they are able to sit up unaided (around 6 months).

That, to my mind, is an ineffective purchase. Parents could have bought a cot that would last two years for this child and each subsequent children for the same amount of money, and it would have made no difference to the welfare of the baby.

> **TOP TIP: BUY THINGS THAT WILL GROW WITH YOUR CHILD**
>
> Use the travel cot as an example. Ask yourself how long you want to use each product
> for. Do you expect it to grow with your child? Why not ask if there are other products that
> do the same as the one you are researching but which can be adapted to suit other uses
> when your child grows.

EXCRETING

There's no great way to say this or read about it but baby poo will rapidly become an everyday occurrence (several times a day, in fact), so it's important you get to grips with how you intend to approach it (other than from the other side of the room with a nose clip).

Practically speaking, newborn babies poo an enormous amount. There will be a smelly nappy to clean up 10 minutes after each feed and probably another one in between. However, after a month or so, a baby's digestion settles down a little and then you're onto between six and eight wet or dirty nappies a day (as a rough estimate).

The big question is whether to go organic and opt for reusable terry nappies or whether to go down the disposable route.

❝❝ I did put Edward in terry nappies and it worked fine. It probably helped that [husband] Jon was willing to go along with it. We had a two bucket system: one for wee nappies and one for poo. They'd soak for a day or so and then be washed at 60 degrees. Wash-wise, it meant two extra loads a week and I did feel very virtuous hanging them out on the line. I gave up with Arwenna and put her in disposable nappies because the cloth nappies were too bulky and her clothes just didn't fit properly. And with 2 children already, George went straight into disposables. But I remember the whole system we had going, it really wasn't difficult to do and I suppose it worked out cheaper. ❞❞

Beth, mother to Edward, Arwenna and George

Whether you choose disposable or re-usable nappies, one thing is certain: your child will use an average of seven nappies a day for between two and three years (once the newborn weeks are over). That's about 2,500 nappies a year or 6,250 nappies until they're toilet trained.

Cost

The cost of disposable nappies is largely hidden. They can be bought in the weekly supermarket shop so the cost is absorbed into general household expenditure. The cost of re-usable nappies, on the other hand, can be off-putting because it is an up-front cost and therefore a big bill.

However, in order to make a reasoned decision, these costs need to be compared side by side. There is a wealth of information available on the cost of real vs disposable nappies from both **www.babykind.co.uk** and the Women's Environmental Network (**www.wen.org.uk**).

Just as there are many types of disposable nappies, so there are many brands of eco-nappies available and the costs vary considerably.

Basic terry nappies are cheap. Yet, as Beth found out (on the previous page) when she had a girl, they don't always fit snugly around the bottom so clothes don't always fit over them. Other reusable nappies are shaped better but naturally cost more.

The choice of which type of nappy to clad your baby's bottom in is not just an environmental one. Some parents can afford a large outlay to save the planet; others will rely on the weekly Child Benefit to finance any nappy and formula requirements they have. To help that decision making process, I've laid bare the full and frank costs of some of these options.

 TOP DEAL

ASDA OWN BRAND, 6.9 PENCE EACH

Total cost of using disposable nappies (using an average price of 7.5p per nappy) based on two and a half years' use.

The own brand baby	The designer baby
Nappies (@7.5p a nappy) £470	Nappies (@12p a nappy) £750
Wipes (@£2 a week) £260	Wipes (@ £3 a week) £380
Total £730	**Total £1,130**

Disposable nappies

Nappies, without discounts, come in at around 15p each for branded type (Pampers, Huggies) or less than 10p each for supermarket-brand varieties.

In their battle for our purses, supermarkets increasingly offer great bargains on disposable nappies. I researched which supermarket had the best offers at the time I wrote this chapter. The answer, that week, was Asda. However, as with all supermarket offers, it is worth checking regularly and stocking up online or in store when a good deal comes up.

 TOP DEAL

By using **www.mysupermarket.co.uk**, I found Asda offered the best value nappies at the time I conducted my research. Their best offers were:

- **Huggies**: A bulk pack of 108 nappies sold for £8, averaging 7.5p each.
- **Pampers**: Asda's offer of three packs for £10 meant 81 nappies (enough for 11 days) cost £10, averaging 12p each.
- **Own Brand**: Asda's offer of three packs for £10 meant I could buy 144 nappies (three weeks' supply) for £10, averaging 6.9p each.

Reusable nappies

Each kit requires different things, but the broad costs of three main types of re-usable nappies have been summarised here. Basically, terry nappies are the bulky old-fashioned variety that are folded to fit. One-size, shaped nappies are exactly that – more shaped, so they are less bulky than terry nappies but still bulkier than multi-sized systems. Regardless of which system you use, most experts recommend that you buy 21 washable nappy elements: enough for three days so two days' worth can be washed and dried during day three. Depending on the system you choose, you may also need plastic over-pants and liners, which can be flushed away along with any solids.

Terry nappies	Mother-ease one sized, shaped, two-part systems	Multi-sized pocket systems (source: www.babykind.co.uk)
Boots terry nappies (£10 for six) = £40	21 one size nappies = £120	Based on 21 nappies, choosing to use FuzziBunz pocket nappies exclusively will cost you £725.97 including inserts.
Boots waterproof pants (£3 for five) = £12	21 ultra fleece liners = £44.10	
Nappy pins (pack of six) = £1.50	4 wraps per size (£32 for four pack per size)= £64	However, large pocket nappies dry very quickly. So, a comfortable number of each size would be 21 small, 18 medium and 15 large nappies. This would reduce the cost to a more realistic £589.20.
Liners (£2.50 for 100) = £22.50	Liners (£2.50 for 100) = £22.50	
Total cost = £76	**Total cost = £250.60**	
Total cost with wipes (at £2 a week) = £336.00	**Cost including wipes = £510.50**	**Total cost £589.20**
	However, using the Mother-ease Sandy two-size system would mean using 21 small nappies, 18 large nappies, 21 boosters, and 21 fleece liners, bringing the cost to **£420.24**	**Total cost including wipes (at £3 a week for brand names) = £969.60**
	Cost including wipes = £680.24	

(Source: www.babykind.co.uk)

So, to put things into perspective, only the most expensive designer versions of reusable nappies cost more than the cheapest version of disposable nappies.

However, this does not take into account the cost of running two extra loads of washing a week. The Women's Environmental Network (WEN) estimates that this could increase the costs by **£133 over two and a half years** (factoring in machine depreciation, detergent and electricity).

(£) TOP DEAL

The nearly-new section of my local **www.netmums.com** website had some fantastic nappy bargains.

- **20 Kissaluvs nappies and three wraps** in size zero (would suit babies up to age 6 months). Set would cost £80–£90 new, but was selling for £10.

Saving £70

- **A full set of Bambino Mio reusable nappies** comprising 24 size one cotton nappies, 24 size two cotton nappies and the following nappy covers: four newborn, three small, four medium, three large, three extra large and 300 throw away liners. A complete kit for any child from birth to age two would have cost £225 new, but was selling for £35.

Saving: £190

Getting the car right

If you need a car, or indeed if you already have a car, think about whether it will work as a family vehicle. If it doesn't, trade it in, now, while you still have the savings to do so.

This might seem a rather drastic measure. After all you've only acquired a baby and they're only small aren't they?

TOP TIP: BUY THE BIGGEST CAR YOU CAN AFFORD TO RUN

A friend of ours, Lloyd, suggested that we should buy the biggest car we could afford (new or secondhand) when he found out we were expecting. It was great advice. We bought a five-year old estate car and used every inch of space imaginable. We never once believed such a small person could need so much stuff!

I fully remember packing up our car to visit the grandparents. It felt like we were packing for an expedition to the Antarctic with the amount of stuff we took along.

As a theoretical exercise – and before you actually need to travel with a great deal of kit – open the boot of your car. Now try and fit the following items in comfortably.

- Travel cot
- Pram
- Shopping bags
- Suitcase or two travel bags (if grandparents live more than two hours' drive away)

Most small hatchbacks and economical run-arounds (ie the type of cars you might have before children) would struggle to accommodate both a travel cot and a pram. As for shopping as well, forget it. So, if you can't fit all of those items in with ease, it's time to ditch your old Mini Cooper and choose something more practical.

You need a car that's economical but will also have a sizeable boot. That doesn't mean you have to rush out to your nearest car dealer and buy a new car. Why not find something about three or four years old that will serve your family well for another five years. Yes, you could opt for a big, brash (and expensive) 4x4 or MPV, but why not save your pennies and choose an option that will cost only a fraction more than the trade-in price of your existing car:

- Ford Focus
- Ford Mondeo
- Toyota Corolla (or the MPV version, the Corolla Verso)
- Renault Megane (which also comes in a seven-seater version)
- Citroen C4
- Any Volvo estate

Now you have wheels (and hopefully, having read Chapter 1 you have a decent but cheap pram for your little darling too), it's time to consider the minefield that is going out and about.

Out and about

Many new parents spend so long packing up and leaving their house on their first few expeditions with their baby that they are thoroughly exhausted and running woefully late before they've even gone anywhere.

For some reason these days, manoeuvring a baby takes the organisational skills of a military exercise. It shouldn't, of course. The trick is to know what is essential for going out and about and what is, quite simply, either surplus to requirements or a complete waste of money.

PACKING FOR A BABY ON THE MOVE

Unless going out means popping to the shops on foot for half an hour, parents of new babies need to take a lot of kit with them. For this, retailers are practically falling over themselves to offer nappy changing bags the size of a paratroopers' rucksack that cost a fortune. Yes, I'm sure the bags offered by the likes of Boden, Blooming Marvellous and indeed Bugaboo (whose colours coordinate with the pram) are lovely, but they are so unnecessary. They retail at between £40 and £75: money which could be put to better use.

The idea of a changing bag, however, is fantastic. Just don't get caught up in the baby-hype when choosing.

You need:

- Three separate pockets: one for dirty/soiled clothes/nappies; one for milk/food; and one for clean nappies/wipes/clothes
- A front pocket to carry purse/wallet/phone and keys is also a good idea
- A waterproof pocket for the milk/food
- A baby changing mat that can fold up

Specialist baby changing bags often have one pocket that is insulated and will therefore keep milk bottles at the ideal temperature. However, supermarkets and baby shops sell bottle insulators for a fraction of the price of baby changing bags and they can be used in whatever bag you choose.

TOP TIP: ADAPT AN EXISTING RUCKSACK/HANDBAG

All the while large handbags are in, why not save £50 and put an existing rucksack or big handbag to good use? Simply place a plastic bag in one compartment for your insulated bottles and carry on as normal. It will serve the same purpose. (It certainly did when my two were small and I still use the handbags today.)

Understandably, not everyone has a large handbag or wants to use it for such a purpose (particularly dads). So, if you wish to invest in a changing bag, make sure it is one that can be used comfortably by both sexes. There's no need to fork out £55 on the DadGear backpack just so that he doesn't get embarrassed using your pink nylon contraption. Choose a neutral bag that can clip on to the pushchair and comes with a bottle-insulating pouch and a changing mat and you're away.

 TOP DEAL

I searched for a Bugaboo changing bag online.

- Bugaboo changing bags cost an eye watering £75 new
- The same Bugaboo bag – new – sold on eBay for £41 plus £5 p&p
- However, there was also a mint condition Bugaboo bag selling for a fixed price of £10.50 with free delivery, also from eBay. Bargain.

Total saving: £65

- Another great find was the Petit Planet baby changing rucksack on Amazon. co.uk Marketplace for £7.
- A robust bag that is built to last and is good for both mums and dads is the Samsonite baby backpack. They retail at £35.
- An e-retailer on eBay had the same new bag available for £17 plus free delivery.

Total saving £18

Parents rapidly realise that excursions invariably take longer than planned and babies will choose the moment when you're as far away from home/milk/spare nappies as possible to either develop an extreme thirst, extreme hunger, or extreme need for clean nappies. So, for a day trip, plan to take:

- Nappies, nappy sacks and pocket wipes
- At least one change of clothes
- Two bottles of infant or expressed milk (there may not be breast feeding options on the move!)
- One measured portion of formula and a baby bottle with the measured amount of water for mixing
- Two muslin squares (they serve all kinds of functions, not least as an emergency fifth nappy should you run out!)

That will be enough for 6 hours out and about plus a contingency for unexpected delays (such as a motorway pile-up).

Now you and your baby are mobile it's time to work out where you can go without breaking the bank.

Filling the days with fun

Looking after a young child can be fun, exciting and rewarding. It can also be monotonous and you can feel the brain cells popping one by one as you spend another day watching *This Morning* and *In the Night Garden* or singing along to the *Tweenies* theme tune.

BIRTH TO SIX MONTHS

At this stage, your child will find anything interesting, particularly if surrounded by the hubbub of conversation and lots of bright lights. Meeting up with friends for a cup of coffee once a week will achieve that. It will give you a reason to leave the house wearing clean clothes and having taken a shower, and you'll appreciate the adult company. However, even sane refreshing adult company comes at a cost: a £3 a week coffee shop excursion will cost more than £150 a year.

One great way to get out and about is to combine exercise with a bit of baby bonding. All new mothers need to get back into shape and there are various ways of doing this.

The cheap option

I joined a post-natal fitness class run by a great lady called Sue in an old dusty church hall. The hall had a side room where she organised a crèche. As we kept fit once a week, the babies grew from gurgling at each other to crawling over one another to kicking a football around together. It combined exercise, camaraderie and friendship for the mothers and the babies alike. After the class we'd sit for half an hour with a cup of tea and a biscuit while the babies came in and joined us. It was significantly cheaper than a gym and I made lifelong friends. (Cost: around £5 a week.)

The free option

If a fiver a week is simply not an option, why not get your own circle of mothers together for a once-a-week walk/jog around the park? You get fresh air and exercise and could round it all off nicely with a sociable cuppa. You could each take turns to host the post-exercise chit chat.

The expensive options

Post-natal fitness classes for mums and bumps are run in a variety of places, from the local park to your nearest private gym. They can cost as much as £10 a session (£40–£50 a month). Losing the baby tummy can become an issue for many mums and, for those who want to shape up in a way that suits their body, a personal trainer might be the answer. Expect to pay £25–£30 per session.

SIX TO 12 MONTHS

Once your baby is sitting up, the world becomes much more exciting (which means more of a challenge for you). Life with a little one is as much about relieving the monotony as it is about providing new experiences. At this stage, playgroups may not be the answer (wait until your little one is walking or crawling with much more confidence) as there are some boisterous toddlers about. Instead, look at other options. Here are a few ideas to ensure you're out and about doing something different with your little one every day.

The cheap options

1. **Set a weekly play date with the antenatal friends.** Take it in turns to host. If the children are only just sitting and you have wood, laminate or stone floors, put a duvet on the floor covered in cushions to provide a bit of padding. At this stage, the babies just want a change of scene and the idea of being with other babies will appeal, even if they don't interact. It will also give mums the chance to swap notes and catch up.

2. **Check out your local library.** Many libraries have weekly story time. Some divide this into different age groups so that the pre-schoolers (those aged between three and five) get different stories from the really young. Even if you've already done story time that week, the library makes a great wet day activity. It's warm, it's dry, it's child friendly and there are other children for your little one to interact with.

3. **Feed the ducks.** Believe it or not, a simple trip to a river bank to feed the ducks counts as an outing. Yes, you could very well slot it onto the back of another activity but why do that when it can be enjoyed as an activity on its own?

4. **Go to the playground.** Most people have a playground nearby. If you

live in a busy area or one with nearby schools, you could have a choice
of several. If you do, then why not have two playground days a week
and alternate which ones you go to? Each will have slightly different
activities and each will be geared to a slightly different age group, but
keeping to a routine while injecting a bit of variety is key at this age.

5.   **Take a bus or train ride.** You don't have to go very far, or even have
a particularly good reason for travelling, but instead of going by car,
why not take the bus or go by train? Children adore public transport.
They love seeing all the other passengers and/or watching out of high
windows whilst sitting on your knee. Even if you decide to take a trip
just to buy a pint of milk, that counts as an outing in itself. To avoid
turning an outing into a stressful experience, don't travel in the rush
hour or between 3pm and 4pm, when the schools finish. After all, you
want to be able to get on the bus comfortably without being squashed
or shoved.

6.   **Visit the charity shop.** As I explained on page 29 this is a great activity
for children of all ages, whether it is wet or dry, winter or summer.
Children can have a good look around the toys and books and you
won't feel too awful indulging them. After all, if the toy they fell in love
with a week earlier has lost its allure, does it matter if it only cost 50p?

❝❝ We try to get all toys, DVDs and books online at Amazon.
co.uk or Book People etc as it's cheaper. We also always check
the video and DVD shelves in the charity shops – you never
know what you're going to find. As for clothes, we get most
of them in end of season sales. That way we can afford nicer
brands like Boden, Monsoon etc without breaking the bank.
The basics come from Sainsbury's or Primark. ❞❞

Katy, mother of Daisy and Jack

The expensive options
Swimming
Babies can go swimming from around three months. What's more, many
of them (although not all) love every second of it and swimming is great
for their muscle development and motor control, never mind the fact that
learning to swim is a life skill.

There are two ways to do this: either parent and baby swimming classes, where an instructor will teach you how to handle your baby in the water and things they find fun, or just turn up at the local pool and enjoy the water with your little one. Clearly classes cost more, but for those who either feel nervous about handling their child in a big expanse of water, or who like the structure of an advice-based session, it is one of the few activities at this age that is value for money. For those who are confident, going alone with your child is a great option. Just make sure baby has a swim nappy on.

Hobbies

I shudder to use the word 'hobby' when referring to a one year old, but, like it or not, there is a whole industry out there geared up to taking your hard earned money from you in order to give your baby an interest. They include things like:

- □ Tumble Tots
- □ Baby gym
- □ Monkey Music
- □ Jo Jingles
- □ Baby yoga
- □ Baby signing
- □ Baby singing

These weekly activities can cost around £60 for a 12-week term, which is akin to what a full-blown hobby for a school-age child might cost. So, before you enrol your little Baby Mozart up to a term's tambourine bashing, ask yourself whether it's a good idea first.

If money were no object then, of course, some of these activities might be really good. However, before you sign up to any of them, make sure you can attend a trial class with your child and see what you are getting for the money. If you cannot get a trial lesson, don't part with any cash because you cannot see whether the format suits you and your little one.

> ### (£) TOP DEAL
>
> Yes, OK, this sounds cheap and it probably is, but there's nothing wrong with sampling a variety of classes to see which your child prefers before signing up with any of them (or not at all, as the case may be). If you are questioned about whether you intend to commit to any of these classes, you can always say you're having a detailed look to see which of the music classes (Jo Jingles, Monkey Music, Baby Singing, Musical Madness, Music Bugs etc) your child prefers. You'll get a far better idea of which one offers value for money by trialling them all, than by just picking the first option from your local area website. What's more, it'll probably take you the best part of a term to do all the research, saving you a term's fees. Result.
>
> **Total saving: around £60**

Feeding

Food is not an issue for the first four to six months of your baby's life. It's milk, milk, milk all the way, whether it comes from breast or bottle. When food finally comes on the menu, it is astonishing how much you can spend on such a tiny person who eats so little.

> ### TOP TIP: KEEP JARS FOR EMERGENCIES ONLY
>
> Ignore jars except in emergencies. Make your own baby food instead. It may only take one hour a week to prepare, is organic, fresh and cheap.

Of course pre-made meals in jars have their uses, especially when you are caught out and about with a hungry, grumpy, loud bundle of misery and only a jar from Boots or the motorway services will do. By and large, however, home-made is cheaper and better. In fact, other than the cost of a box of baby rice once a fortnight, there should be no additional food costs over and above your weekly shopping bill.

FEEDING YOUR BABY FOR JUST ONE HOUR'S WORK A WEEK

When my son was small I got into a great routine which worked so well, I slipped straight back into it again when it was my daughter's turn to be weaned.

I boiled or steamed vegetables on a Sunday, blended them one type at a time, and poured the resultant goo into ice cube trays. In the early days, bland vegetables such as sweet potato and carrot were all that was needed. After a month or so, I could add a few more varieties. In the end I probably steamed and blended half a dozen different vegetables each week and, as my children got bigger, so the blending got rougher and rougher.

Home feeding equipment
- A blender
- Three ice cube trays
- A steamer (optional – you can steam using a saucepan and colander)
- Plastic bowls with lids (so you can take food with you)

The early days

In the first couple of months, all that a baby will get through is probably 250g of sweet potato and the same of carrots in a week, combined with half a packet (maximum) of baby rice.

One sweet potato	40p
Three carrots	21p
Baby rice (1/2 packet)	83p
Total cost	**£1.44 per week**

So, as you can see, taking the DIY approach to baby food hardly puts a dent in the weekly shopping budget.

Eight to 12 months

Babies will tell you what they want to eat, and the easiest way to discover that is to provide them with a sample of finger foods to try out and see what they go for. It is probably easiest to set aside a portion of your own adult food (provided it has no added salt or sugar) and pulp that down to a suitable consistency. If, however, your diet is unsuitable, you could do worse than use the following list of food as a guide :

One packet of baby rice per week	£1.66
Four carrots	28p
One sweet potato	40p

Broccoli (1/2 dozen florets)	40p
Peas	£1
Baby rusks (1/2 packet)	86p
Pureed apple & pear	50p
Two bananas	16p
Total cost	**£5.26 per week**

For that amount of money, your baby will have more food than they could possibly need (you'll probably be able to feed their friends a couple of times a week for that too). There are also plenty of 'extras' that your child will enjoy at this stage that have such a negligible cost I have not accounted for it. They include things like pasta (which costs less than £1 for a family packet) or bread. Basically, extras would be the odd tiny mouthful of your meal just to taste.

PRE-PREPARED BABY FOOD

The big names in baby food are Cow & Gate, Heinz, Hipp Organic and Organix. Many supermarkets now have their own ranges and there are more and more new entrants into the deluxe organic range of foods. Because there can be a variation in price, I have looked at accommodating a totally organic baby and an entirely non-organic child. Many parents taking the pre-prepared option would probably mix and match.

Six to nine months

Non-organic food	**Organic food**
Breakfast: (1/2 packet cereal mix) 93p	Breakfast:
	(1/2 jar per day costing 35p per jar) £1.40
Lunch and Dinner:	
One jar of age appropriate food (costing 45p each) £6.30	Lunch and Dinner:
	One jar of age appropriate food (costing 60p each) £8.40
Dessert:	
1/2 portion of baby fruit dessert (pack of four) £1.60	Dessert:
	1/2 portion of baby fruit pudding (pack of four) £1.40
Total cost = £8.83 per week	
	Total cost = £11.20 per week

As babies grow, their appetites grow, so the jars of pre-prepared food get bigger and consequently become more expensive.

12 months

Non-organic food	Organic food
Breakfast: One packet cereal mix £1.86	Breakfast: Banana muesli £2.48
Lunch: One jar per meal (costing 87p each) £6.09	Lunch: One jar per meal (costing 90p each) £6.30
Dinner: One prepared meal tray per sitting (costing £1.15 each) £8.05	Dinner: One prepared meal tray per sitting (costing £1.30 each) £9.10
Pudding: 14 portions (costing 50p each) £7	Pudding: 14 portions (costing 50p each) £7
Total cost = £23.00 per week	**Total cost = £24.88 per week**

Spending an hour or so on a Sunday afternoon preparing a week's worth of baby meals may seem like a mindless chore until the numbers are laid bare. Most people have a blender (if you don't, mash the baby food through a sieve with a fork) and, if you don't have a steamer, use a saucepan and just boil the veg. But, in pure economic terms, spending £1.50 on a six-month old infant each week is much more compelling than spending £9 a week.

Going away with baby

I bravely travelled to Sicily with my infant son when he was just six weeks old. Never again. He wasn't yet comfortable in his own skin and I was not yet comfortable enough with the rigours of motherhood to cope with such an upheaval. However, once he was 12 weeks old he settled into a routine and seemed much happier in his surroundings. I was much more confident handling him outside of the home and suddenly it seemed right to be able to venture further afield.

TOP TIP: ONLY TRAVEL WHEN YOU'RE READY

Don't be browbeaten into travelling before you are entirely ready and comfortable doing so. A stressed mum means a stressed baby and a torturous time of it.

Once you feel able to travel (and possibly spend the night) somewhere other than your own home, then it's time to look at what you really need to pack and what you can do without. Here's the essential list to make your life easier on the move.

THINGS FOR THE JOURNEY

- ☐ Change of top for mum and dad
- ☐ Complete change of outfit for baby
- ☐ Complete nappy bag (as above, in 'Out and about'), comprising three milks, two foods (if feeding), four nappies, wipes, nappy sacks and a couple of muslin squares

STAYING IN THE UK OR WITH RELATIVES

The great thing about staying with British-based relatives (or indeed staying anywhere in Britain) is that, if you have a baby emergency, you generally know where to go for supplies. I remember my mother-in-law having our son to stay for a night when he was about three months old. While we caught up on sleep, our son had a raging temperature. His body's way of trying to cool himself down was to be sick – repeatedly and violently. My mother-in-law hadn't wanted to disturb us so she'd battled gamely on. By the time we found out, even though it was Sunday and many shops and pharmacists etc were closed, we still knew where to go to get what we needed.

THE POWER OF CALPOL

It is dangerous to assume that a single spoonful of pink liquid is the answer to every child illness issue. Of course it isn't. However, it can be the answer to a lot of niggly illnesses that can distress your child and therefore worry you. Travel sachets of Calpol are consequently an essential piece of kit for any holidaying family.

Have to pack

- ☐ Calpol
- ☐ Three changes of clothes (wear one, wash one, dry one)
- ☐ Cot sheet and baby blanket
- ☐ A couple of fabric books
- ☐ A couple of toys
- ☐ Milk formula or expressed milk
- ☐ Clean, sterile bottles

- □ Muslin squares (make great dribble cloths, shoulder protectors, emergency clothes, etc)
- □ Stroller or pushchair for walks
- □ Travel cot (if needed)

Nice to have

- □ Bouncy chair or play mat
- □ Kids' story tape, tune or mobile, depending on what equipment is available
- □ Chew toy
- □ Soft toy for cot
- □ Portable booster feeding chair (can use baby bouncer or car seat, if under six months)

I was always guilty of packing too much stuff for my children to 'do', forgetting that, at that age, everything is entertaining and a change of scene is exciting in itself. Two or three small, handbag sized toys are fine. Nothing else is needed.

Other than clothes, which can easily be packed, baby's requirements can be met almost anywhere you'd choose to go. Nappies, formula and food can be acquired anywhere, as can medicine should something go wrong. So long as your baby has somewhere to sleep and you have the ability to provide food and clean clothes, that's all that matters.

HOLIDAYING ABROAD

Once again, firms have understood that we overcompensate when it comes to our children and therefore have a tendency to buy too much. Most mums have regretted buying at least one item when holidaying with their child for the first time.

Some of the regrets (and their costs) are listed below. However, do realise that for every mum who has regretted a particular purchase, there is likely to be another mum who swears by that very same item, regarding it as invaluable.

Pop-up sun shade tent

'I spent £25 on this thing and Katy was never in it. The following year she was too big for it. What a waste of money. Sam never used it either.' Christine, mum to Alex, Katy and Sam

Cost: £20–£45

Baby sunglasses

'Babies don't need sunglasses if they've got a hat with a brim. They have sunglasses to play with them. Then they pull the arms back and snap the hinges. What a waste of money.' Maddy, mum to Arthur and Eve

Cost: £3

Baby wetsuit

'If babies are in their local swimming pool, it's heated and, if not, they're not in the water for long enough to need a wetsuit.' Claire, mum to Hamish and Jack

Cost: £15–£20

The go-anywhere black-out blind

On paper, this is a fantastic idea. In reality, some of the parents I spoke to complained that they were just a bit of a pain – especially if they fell down in the night!

Cost: around £30

6. Toddler and pre-school years

Oh, yes, toddlers: great little balls of joy and unbridled tantrums, put together in fantastic packaging that includes nuclear snot and other unmentionable supposedly biodegradable stains that prove oddly stubborn. Toddlers are noisy and they have a beguiling ability to manipulate circumstances to suit themselves. But they're great fun.

Once your child is between two and five years old, they have probably got to grips with your daily routine and house rules and are busy tweaking and amending these to better fit what they had in mind. That's great: it demonstrates a variety of skills you may find incredibly frustrating in one so small but which you will want your little treasure to possess in spades when it comes to adulthood – negotiation; the ability to think outside the box (toddlers don't know there is a box in the first place) and non-conformist tendencies.

The question, of course, is how to harness this and fulfil your child's potential while not breaking the bank, *and* still give him or her plenty of fun along the way.

Toys

Toys for the toddler years are brilliant. Your children haven't outsmarted you in the technology stakes yet and many of the toys that really light a child's fire are oddly familiar. Names like Lego and Brio resonate as much with today's kids as they did with us a generation ago. So, if you or your parents kept any of your childhood treasures in a box in the attic, now's the time to dust them off and see what has stood the test of time.

Each year toy giants manufacture a whole new range of delights to get everyone spending their hard earned cash at the tills. Some are worth it; others are just the latest fad. So how do you know that what you buy will stand the test of time?

It's time to look at the development of your child and therefore which toys fulfil age-appropriate needs, and also which types of toys will grow with your child.

TOYS THAT GROW WITH YOUR CHILDREN

These toys stand the test of time, primarily because, as children get older, they play with them in different ways.

Train tracks

When a child is between two and three years old, building the train track will be the responsibility of mum or dad. However, by the time that same child is four or five they will be building their own tracks. Sadly, many of these tracks are likely to be in a straight line, so trains will end up under the sofa. But, by five or six, children will be better at building circuits, enabling them to begin to play with the same toy in more complex and intricate ways. When children are junior school age, they can really get to grips with multiple inter-connecting tracks, with crossways, dividers, bridges and level crossings.

Brio tracks are fantastic because they are made from sustainable produce (ie wood), can be passed from generation to generation, and are robust enough to sustain being thrown around the room when your lovely little angel has a house full of equally angelic friends to play. The downside is that Brio tracks are hugely expensive. However, they are a great secondhand find and there are some fantastic, cheaper, imitations that interlink perfectly.

While this toy is most loved by pre-school and infant children, it is still played with by junior age kids.

New	Cheaper imitations	Charity shops/secondhand
John Lewis (www.johnlewis.com) has one of the best selections. A basic first railway set costs £20. Elements including a turntable (£11), station (£30), or battery operated trains (£17) can be added bit by bit.	The **Early Learning Centre's** (www.elc.co.uk) own wooden train track fits neatly with Brio, so different elements will work together. Its Wooden World construction train set contains 70 pieces, priced at £35.	**eBay** is once again great value but, because sellers know the residual value of Brio, items are still pricey. I saw a selection of Brio and ELC track and trains for £30. There was also a selection of advanced track pieces for £11 (usually retails at £20).
Argos (www.argos.co.uk) also has a good selection with advanced track bits, including junctions and cross tracks from £20 a set, a starter pack for £15 and various variations.	**Tesco** (www.tesco.com) also has its own version. It has 56 pieces, including a suspension bridge for a bargain £10.	**NCT** nearly-new sales. Brio train tracks are a regular find at secondhand sales. Expect to pay £10 for a variety of track and trains.
		School fairs. My next door neighbour found all the trains for her track at local primary school fairs. Prices varied from 50p a train to £1 for a bag full of trains.

So on to another great classic, this time from Denmark. That's right: Lego.

Lego

There is more than one type of Lego. There's Lego Brio for little fingers (and to prevent choking and accidents) and there's the regular Lego you and I might remember from our own childhood.

Now there are Star Wars sets, Indiana Jones sets, Lego vehicles, Lego alien fighters called Bionicles, even Lego roof tiles, steering wheels, windscreens and seats. In fact, you name it: Lego produces a particular brick to construct it. Of course, all of this costs money, but, once again, Lego is the sort of toy that turns up time and again at school summer fetes, church hall sales, charity shops and on eBay.

> I bought our boys 5lb of Lego on eBay last year, and 4,500 pieces of K'Nex this year for the holidays. VERY happy kids, and much cheaper than retail so VERY happy parents. We also have friends who regularly shop at Goodwill/Salvation Army

charity shops and have bought lots of great toys for their kids there. 🙿

Monica, US, mother of Noah and Jonah

The other thing about Lego is to choose carefully what sets you buy. Lego Indiana Jones or Star Wars might be all the rage, but when the novelty of playing with specific characters wears off, what else are those pieces going to be turned into? Better to leave specific sets like that for special birthday requests from friends and family and get a hardy tub full of basic pieces that can be turned into anything at the drop of a hat.

New	New bargains	Charity shops/secondhand
John Lewis (www. johnlewis.com) has one of the best selections. The Lego Creator giant box has an astonishing 1,600 bricks of various shapes and sizes for £50. It can be augmented with wheel sets or window and doors for £10 a set. Expensive but will last from age three to age 10. Smaller fingers can get the same fun out of a Lego Duplo bargain bucket: also £50.	Tesco (www.tesco. com) has a whole Lego shop within its online store and plenty of choice in many of the larger superstores. Its bargain bucket (with 216 pieces) costs £13, compared to the next best price of £15 + £4 p&p from The Entertainer (www. thetoyshop.com)	eBay is not necessarily good value here. A 'bargain' bucket cost £24 inc postage here. More than it would have cost from Tesco or The Entertainer. Biggest rip-off was a Lego City Helicopter selling for £12.50 inc p&p when they only cost £10 in the shops! The real bargains were on unpackaged Lego. Half a kilo of Lego for £10 including p&p and a set of cogs and wheels for £8.

GOING SECONDHAND

TOP TIP: GO UPMARKET

The smarter the neighbourhood, the better the quality of secondhand toys but also the sharper the shoppers' elbows!

All local authorities now have websites with details of local primary schools within their catchment area. Nearly all of those schools now have their own websites where they publish key dates. Before you buy anything, check out the dates of Christmas and summer fairs at the local schools in your area and the smartest suburb near to you.

Similarly, go on the NCT website and find nearly-new sales in your area (**www.nctpregnancyandbabycare.com**). Also look at church websites for charity sales or jumble sales. All are fantastic shopping arenas. They tend to be indoors and they tend not to start before 10am or 11am, so they are less antisocial than some car boot sales.

Go armed with cash, go early and be prepared to get stuck in to find your toy bargains.

> ❝ Bowdon Church School PTA secondhand sale! Bargains galore! Boden, GAP clothes and hardly used bikes etc. Also can't beat charity shops in Hale Village! ❞
>
> Caroline, mum to Sam and Sally

Great secondhand finds

Aside from Lego and Brio there are other great secondhand finds that turn up again and again and will last for years.

- **Brick trucks**. Any kind of push-along toy is a developmental must for children between nine months and about two years. Some of them can cost as much as £100 new but they are a regular find in secondhand fairs, so keep your eyes peeled.
- **K'NEX**. Another construction toy, K'NEX is often used in primary schools and is a great way of building all manner of things, from big buildings to imaginary creatures. It will last kids from age five to age 10, so it is great for the whole of primary school.
- **Kiddi K'NEX**. A more user-friendly version of K'NEX, designed for pre-school and infant school-aged engineers. It is colourful, fun, robust and will still be played with from time to time by junior age kids.
- **Climbing frames**. These are more of a car boot find than a school fair find but occasionally you will see one. They turn up because once children have outgrown them, no parent wants to keep them hanging around. A sturdy Little Tikes playhouse

or climbing frame can usually be picked up for about £10 and will last a good five years before you sell it on again.

▫ **Bikes.** Primary school newsletters and shop notice boards are a great way to find a secondhand bike. Usually, bikes, trikes and ride-along bikes that attach to parents' bikes get passed on in excellent condition because children grow out of them before they wear them out. Expect to pay £5–£25 depending on the bike and your local area. Even the most expensive secondhand price is still usually half the price of the cheapest new bike on offer.

▫ **Branded toys.** Things such as Thomas the Tank Engine (a must for boys aged 18 months – four years); Power Rangers (again, a boy toy, this time ages three to five years); Ben 10 (another boy thing, good for infant schoolers); Barbie, Polly Pocket and Bratz dolls and assorted accoutrements (will suit any girl from age four) are all fantastic secondhand bargains. Expect to pay 10% of their original value.

▫ **DVDs and videos.** Shops may no longer sell video recorders but plenty of homes still have old video players, and there is no shortage of videos doing the rounds at school fairs. There are plenty of DVDs around too, from popular kids TV programmes to Disney films, so go and rummage for a bargain. Expect to pay 50p or £1 for a DVD, less for videos.

TOYS FOR FREE

There are shops galore catering to the every whim of your child. Retailers know parents are easy prey because they want to keep their little darlings happy. However, there are plenty of toys that are better to make than to buy: in part because it is so much cheaper, but also because making the toy is part of the fun.

A LESSON LEARNED

One summer holiday when my children were age four and 18 months, we made a castle out of shoeboxes and Lego Duplo as a home for the toy soldiers in the house. It had a central courtyard, battlements and even a staircase (ah, the sturdiness of Lego!). The kids loved making it and it was played with endlessly. Eventually it fell apart. That Christmas, Father Christmas got my son a castle from the Early Learning Centre that had to be assembled. It was great. But it wasn't home-made and so wasn't played with nearly as much as the one we'd created together.

Similarly, we have a home-made barn for the Christmas nativity (another subtly painted shoebox!) and all manner of home-made instruments, from shakers and rainmakers to 'guitars' (I use the term loosely!). None are as shiny as shop bought products or even as able to do what is required of them but all have won in the popularity stakes over the years.

Play dough

Yes, those variety packs of Play-Doh look really enticing in their shiny colours and co-ordinated plastic tubs, but play dough costs nothing to make and you can use (small) quantities of food colouring to make different colours at home. Think how virtuous you will feel having made a toy that is environmentally conscious and does not come in shiny plastic packaging. Also, at least you will know just how edible it is – as small children eating it is inevitable!

Play dough can last for weeks like this, especially if kept in the fridge. However, if it you forget to pack it away and it goes hard this way, it's much cheaper to replace.

Ingredients
1 cup of plain flour
1/2 cup salt
1 cup water with 6 or 7 drops of food colouring added
2 tablespoons vegetable oil
2 tablespoons cream of tartar
1 teaspoon vanilla essence (if you want the play dough to smell nice!)

Simply put all the ingredients into a saucepan and stir over a medium heat until the dough forms into a ball. Allow to cool and then knead until smooth. Play dough can be easily stored either in a freezer bag or a Tupperware container with a sealable lid.

Musical instruments

From rattles to guitars, part of the fun of noisy toys is making them.

Rattles: Simply get a screw top bottle (such as a small water bottle) and half fill it with hard things such as pearl barley, lentils or small pasta shapes. To decorate it, you can paint or colour a design onto a piece of paper and then wrap it around the rattle.

Guitars: Take a shoebox with a lid. Cut a circular hole out of the middle of the lid. Decorate the box and lid how you fancy. Then place a selection of elastic bands around the boxed lid. This may not be music to you but will make a satisfying 'twang' for your toddler.

- Shoeboxes are great for making castles, dolls houses, cars, puppet theatres etc
- Egg boxes make fantastic crocodiles and jewellery boxes
- Pizza bases can be used to make masks (or the bases of buildings)
- Old yoghurt pots can do anything from home made miniature mobiles to paint pots
- Kitchen roll or loo roll inner tubes make fantastic skittles

---

TOP TIP: BUILD UP A CRAFT BOX

When my children went to visit one of their grandmas over the summer they found a stash of craft equipment all ready for them. From the netting used to hold onions or oranges to bottle tops, yoghurt pots and bubble wrap, my mum had carefully collected this over a period of months so that the children could paint, glue and create to their hearts' content. For paint, they used old decorating sample tins (water-based emulsion, obviously) and for paper? That was the ends of old wallpaper rolls.

Making a craft box

Primary schools use recycled materials all the time in their craft activities so why not take a leaf out of their book?

Suitable items include: shoeboxes, cereal boxes, old milk cartons, shiny sweet paper, yoghurt pots, lids, foil bases, pizza bases, and drink bottles. Old bits of fabric, ribbons, sheets or torn pairs of trousers can also come in handy. Simply think of all the *Blue Peter* moments you either watched or participated in during your own childhood and draw on that to make your own craft collection.

CHILD DEVELOPMENT AND TOYS

Most shop bought toys come with an age label. The temptation, in these days of ultra-achievement, is to assume your child is a prodigy if they are playing with a toy above their own age or, more worryingly, to assume your child has learning issues if their favourite toy is 'young' for them. Nothing could be further from the truth. Some toys might say 'suitable from 18 months' but that does not necessarily mean you should avoid buying that toy for a child's second or third birthday present. Children re-visit toys as their cognitive and motor skills develop and therefore can play with the same item in many different ways.

Having a house bursting at the seams with a wealth of toys doesn't make for a more advanced or even more stimulated child. In fact, too much choice can sometimes engender anxiety or lack of concentration as children are either overwhelmed by the choice on offer or feel they must play with everything on offer. The best way to help your child, and get value for money out of your toys, is to know what toys are best suited to which infant development stage.

One to two years
- Shape sorters
- Simple jigsaws (four or six-piece puzzles),
- Stacking toys
- Matching
- Grouping
- Texture (especially in nature: leaves, grass, mud, bark, water)
- Action toys
- Simple instruments for rhythm and beat

Two years plus

- Dressing up
- Soft toys/dolls
- Music
- Simple hammer & peg toys to improve fine motor skills and co-ordination
- Farm sets – to help with imagination, scenarios, and playing with others
- Picture dominoes – help establish rule of play, team-working, grouping and cognitive skills
- Jigsaws – 12-piece puzzles

Three years plus

- Beads/jewellery – helps with fine motors skills and concentration
- Home play (kitchen, shop etc) – helps with fine motor skills and mental agility
- Art & craft
- Riding toys – trikes, tractors, anything with wheels
- Tools/work bench – developing on from hammer and peg based toys (although they will still be enjoyed)
- Shape matching, numbers and balance – items such as an abacus, scales (for balance and counterbalance) and simple games that explore these concepts

Four years plus

- Money games – playing shops
- Cooking
- Soft toys
- Toy clocks – starting with learning the hours, then half hours, then quarter hours and finally the five minute intervals in between
- Gardening toys
- Art & craft
- Music – rattle and beat toys remain popular but other 'blowing' instruments can be added

　　　□　Water play – it's the ideal age for exploring relative volumes:
　　　　　how to fill and pour, how to retrieve items from the bottom
　　　　　of a water-filled container etc. Water games constantly test
　　　　　motor and cognitive skills.

Pre-school

Before your child was of pre-school age, there were only four childcare
options to consider:

　　　□　Be a stay at home parent
　　　□　Nursery
　　　□　Childminder/grandparents
　　　□　Nanny

Now that your child has reached pre-school age, there is another option to
consider: local pre-school education.

Pre-schools and nursery schools generally follow one of two patterns:

　　　□　Either they are pre-schools attached to the local state primary
　　　　　whereby your child will socialise with other children within the
　　　　　catchment area but will have to apply for their primary school
　　　　　place afresh,
　　　□　Or they are specialist nursery/pre-schools which your child
　　　　　can attend, but they are not linked to any specific primary
　　　　　school within the area.

Some nurseries attached to schools are free. Privately run nurseries are not.
The government does fund a number of sessions for pre-school age children.
How many sessions and for how long varies from nursery to nursery but it is
usually between two and three sessions each week for children over the age
of three. Parents should check what the position is with each local nursery.

Both types of nursery are only available for a certain number of hours
during the day (usually two or three hours). So for parents who wish to
remain working, they can either consider keeping their child at nursery or
with a childminder for continuity of care and general simplicity, or they can
arrange wrap-around care that will plug the gaps left by holidays, inset days,
remaining working hours etc.

No matter what the decision that has been made, there are educational guidelines laid down by Ofsted (and the appropriate bodies in Scotland, Northern Ireland and Wales) that carers should be following so that your child's education and emotional development remains consistent with his or her peer group. Studies have shown that children who learn within a school or nursery environment at this age develop a good basis of early learning before they start school and become well prepared for the learning that's ahead of them.

Regardless of the educational and emotional journey you choose for your child, there are some questions you should ask:

- What activities do the children do?
- How many children regularly attend? On what days?
- How is the average day or session organised?
- What resources and equipment do you have to support the children's learning?
- How are activities planned and organised to meet the Early Years Foundation Stage?
- Do you provide any additional help for children aged under five with special needs?
- How do staff manage children's behaviour, especially when they misbehave?
- What qualifications and experience do the staff have?
- Are there outdoor and indoor play areas for children?
- Is there a period of rest incorporated into the day?
- What time do sessions start and finish?
- Are there particular schools that children within this pre-school environment go on to attend?

These questions should be asked whether you are assessing a pre-school, playgroup, a childminder, nursery, pre-school attached to a primary school, or children's centre. The answers will help to establish in your mind which provides the best value education in terms of experiences, social skills and environment that will best equip your child to face primary school intellectually, socially and emotionally.

Holidays

Whether or not your little one is school age, there are ways of making sure that your family can have a great holiday without breaking the bank. Camping is cheaper than staying in a hotel or apartment and house swapping is cheaper still. House swapping with relatives, or even staying with them, can ensure (depending on your family relationships) you can have a home-from-home experience that gives you and your family a break from the everyday without going into debt.

TOP TIP: GO OFF PEAK WHILE YOU STILL CAN

Until your child(ren) are school age, make the most of off-peak holiday prices by taking then away in term times. Prices can nearly double once you're restricted to the same six weeks in July and August as everyone else.

Here are some of the best ways of getting a great family holiday.

VALUE-FOR-MONEY HOLIDAYS

Take a winter holiday in summer

We all know that skiing holidays are expensive, but those same deluxe chalets can lie idle and underused during the summer months, ready and waiting for families to take advantage of glorious mountainous, walking holidays. Sure, areas such as the Tyrol remain expensive even in summer but places like the Pyrenees can be great value.

House-swapping

House swapping costs nothing (except the agency fee). It's also nothing new – it has been going for the best part of half a century, it's just that it has taken the British press a while to catch on to what a successful formula it has become. The idea is that people lodge details of their houses or flats with an agency, along with details of the location and type of accommodation they need. Those who take the plunge and opt for a house swapping vacation tend to be repeat customers. That's because, aside from the agency fee, there are no accommodation costs to pay.

Homeowners can swap either within the UK or elsewhere. They simply have to find their way to the property of their choice and stump up for everyday expenses during their stay. It can be a preferable way of holidaying for families because they can trade with other families around the world with kids of similar ages, to ensure the property they stay in is suitable for their needs.

Costs are not always the main criteria for those looking to house swap though. Caroline Connolly, of the agency HomeLink International, says other factors such as the wider comforts and amenities of using someone's home may also appeal, as does the possibility of forging new friendships with other families overseas.

Potential home swappers are encouraged to draw up a shortlist of properties they like the look of before sending a message expressing interest. It's important for those looking to home swap to be honest about their house, its location, facilities, size, layout etc and how they intend items such as phone calls to be paid for. It is also important to be realistic about what your house may offer others as well as what you are looking for in a holiday yourselves.

HOW TO SWAP

HomeLink International (www.homelink.org.uk) has been going for more than 50 years and is one of the longest established home swap agencies in the marketplace with a string of testimonials and – more importantly – a wide geographical reach.

Holiday with friends

While you might want to take a break with your nearest and dearest and wave goodbye to everything that's familiar for a couple of weeks, it can make sense to holiday with friends for all manner of reasons, not least economic ones.

If you are going to hire a holiday home here or abroad, it is cheaper per head to hire one single big place than several small ones. Holidaying with friends is not reserved for twenty-somethings on their gap years. Many families who meet at antenatal classes when pregnant become firm friends and do, indeed, holiday together as families: the children have grown up together, ensuring that they are entertained with much less effort on the part of the parents. Parents also get a greater break, because they are sharing the childcare burden between a greater number of adults.

> ❝❝ We've been on holiday with the same family now for the last four years and are going again this summer to Greece. It's worked because the children get on well and we get on as adults. We're careful to take our time each year and talk about where we want to go, what we expect to do there and how much we want to spend. We're also careful to choose accommodation that gives us our privacy as well as enabling us to be sociable. All in all, it's been a successful formula and the kids love having each other to play with. ❞❞
>
> Jacky, mum to Natasha

Camping

There's camping and there's camping. Do not despair if the idea of pitching a tent brings you out in a cold rash: have you seen the prices of Eurocamp holidays? Here you can have a holiday in a static caravan or a pre-pitched tent in many of the smartest areas in Europe for a fraction of the cost of a conventional holiday in the same areas. The tents are cheaper than the caravans and are fantastic value for money. They have cooking and fridge facilities, a dining area, two or three bedrooms with proper beds, on sites with great pools and other facilities. The tents even have wardrobes! So, for those who want a good value holiday without losing too many home comforts, these are tents that can cater to most people's whims.

Of course camping for real is even cheaper still. The trick is to identify which type of camper you are before embarking on a fortnight's break beneath the canvas.

> ❝❝ We had a fantastic time at Eurocamp last year and have just booked to go again this summer. Max and Lottie both really enjoyed it. The facilities were of a reasonable standard, the whole holiday was great value and there was plenty for the children to do. Because of the location we could also get out and about and explore the local area. It was a great time. ❞❞
>
> Miranda, mum to Max and Charlotte

EXCHANGE RATES MATTER

No, it doesn't matter whether you have a degree in economics or just a great big dollop of common sense: timing with holidays is everything.

Take the US dollar and the British pound. At the height of the credit crunch, the dollar soared in value and became worth almost as much as a pound. The previous year, Brits could get $2 for every £1. That made accommodation, car hire, theme park entry, food and drink half the cost in real terms.

This is significant because the purchasing power of many of the major currencies (such as the dollar and the euro) is roughly akin to the pound. So a dollar will buy about the same in the US as a pound over here. Getting two dollars for every pound therefore makes spending money stretch twice as far as when the dollar and pound are of equivalent value.

> *"Three years ago when the pound was strong against the euro, we holidayed in Portugal. A year later, when there was more than $2 for every £1, we holidayed in the US. Then, in 2009, when both the euro and the dollar had risen strongly against the pound, we ventured further afield. Factoring in the cost of flights, the cost of spending money, accommodation, car hire and everything, each of our holidays ended up costing the same. Most of this benefit is down to exchange rates."*
>
> *Maddy*

Buying a vacation in a resort where the pound is strong can ensure a great value holiday.

CASH IN THOSE LOYALTY POINTS

Tesco Clubcard

Tesco have entered into Clubcard agreements with more and more providers, including various holiday companies. Clubcard vouchers have always been better value when used for mini breaks, days out or treats as opposed to money-off shopping, not least because they generally yield four times their face value when used with third party suppliers.

These days, holidaymakers can cash in their vouchers with the likes of Butlins, Cosmos, Virgin Holidays, Eurotunnel, and Eurocamp rival Siblu, to name a few. A typical family of four – if they saved all their points – could end up saving £200–£300 off the cost of their summer holiday. Not to be sniffed at.

TOP TIP: VOUCHERS CAN MAKE GOING ABROAD AFFORDABLE

Getting a discount of £200–£250 off the cost of a family holiday can mean the difference between making a trip abroad affordable or not. Even if the idea of taking a Cosmos or Butlins holiday with every other Tesco customer doesn't appeal, why not use the vouchers to get a free Eurostar crossing so that you can rent a villa (with friends, to cut the cost, of course) of your choice?

However, there are many ways that Clubcard vouchers can help the family finance throughout the year so, if none of the holidays appeal, don't feel cheated. They can be used for general out-and-about family expenses, so are never going to go to waste.

Nectar points

Those who shop at Sainsbury, Argos, eBay and Amazon.co.uk can earn valuable Nectar points, which can also be put towards the cost of a holiday. For example:

- ◻ 500 points will give you £2.50 off the cost of a Eurostar ticket
- ◻ 200 points will give you £10 off the cost of a holiday or flights with expedia.co.uk
- ◻ You can also get £10 off hotel stays for every 2,000 points

---

MAKE THE HOLIDAY AGE-APPROPRIATE

I have heard of so many parents who have taken their one and two year old children to Disneyland Paris (or, perish the thought, Disneyland itself). At that age, the children won't remember what they have witnessed. That is a holiday for the parents, not the children.

Of course, this applies to days out as much as full-blown holidays.

> ❞❞ When we took Jack to Whipsnade Zoo at the age of two, he was more interested in the cars in the car park than the animals. It had cost a fortune and, in all honesty, it was wasted on him. ❞❞
>
> Claire, mum to Jack and Hamish

In a similar vein I have seen parents with very young children tackle the wonders of Legoland. There is nothing a one year old can really do there and two year olds are limited in their activities but, once children reach the age of three, the world of Legoland opens up to them. At around £30 per entry ticket you want the experience to be worthwhile!

Other themed days out such as Diggerland are also best enjoyed by children aged at least three.

7. Siblings and home economics

Once you're a parent, having a second child is easy, right? One could even say it's child's play!

Not necessarily.

> ❝ Having two children was more than twice the work of having one. ❞
>
> Terri, mum to Rachel and Madeline

Juggling work commitments around one child is a lot easier than trying to do the same around two children. If you are considering childminders or nurseries for more than one child, then your expenditure increases exponentially while your income is unlikely to do anything great.

Then there is the increased emotional and physical strain having more children places on the family unit. Children can enter a whole new realm of challenging behaviours. If you're lucky, they will run tantrums in a tag team formation. If you're unlucky they'll do it at the same time. Even better, they'll do it in public just to show the world you have no control.

There's also the possibility that your children won't necessarily like one another: they might be jealous of the affection and attention you show their sibling or the older child might resent the arrival of the younger one and blame them for disrupting the existing, familiar family dynamics.

Luckily, being the happy, well adjusted adults we all are, we know most of these issues manage to work themselves out.

This chapter is not going to look at the emotional dynamics of siblings. It is here to address the financial implications that having more than one child places on the family unit.

Clothing

It might sound like common sense but, if your first child is a girl, don't opt for a pink pushchair, car seat or pram. Any little brothers that come along later aren't going to thank you when you show them baby photos of themselves swaddled in bubblegum shades from birth.

While most parents think practically about such big ticket items, they don't think so clearly about the smaller issues.

> ❝ We didn't go mad on pink but even so there are items that I regretted buying in that colour once George had come along. I should have stopped to think a bit more. For example, we got Molly a pink Nintendo DS. We should have got a black or white one because then we could have passed it on to George when he was old enough. He won't want to walk around with a pink one! ❞
>
> Michelle, mum to Molly and George

There are certain essential clothes, for example, that can very easily pass from brother to sister (and vice versa) provided they're not either too heavy on the army camouflage print or too heavy on pink, lilac and glitter. They would include:

- Trousers – especially jeans
- Coats
- Pre-walker shoes

- □ Hats and gloves
- □ Pushchair cosytoes or pram blankets
- □ Jumpers and zip-up hoodies
- □ Cot bedding
- □ Beakers/bottles/cutlery etc

Girls can do very nicely in blue with pink accessories such as t-shirts and socks. Likewise, just because your first child is a boy doesn't mean you rush out and buy bedding covered in tractors and diggers. If that is what lights your son's fire, then buy a set of bedroom wall transfers or drawer handles that can be easily changed but ensure everything you could pass on to another child is as gender neutral as possible.

Girls and boys alike look fine and dandy in blue, brown, yellow, red, green and black and white. It doesn't make girls any less feminine to go without pink in their infant years – they will come to it (or not) in their own time.

CLOTHING SWAPS

Most mothers make at least one really good friend at antenatal classes, not least because you go through the same life-changing experiences at roughly the same time. So, make an agreement. If one of you has a boy and one has a girl, agree to exchange all your baby clothes if you have second children and they are of the opposite sex. Most parents I know have got a clothes swap deal going with at least one friend.

> *"I had a boy first; one of my antenatal friends had a girl. We agreed to exchange clothes if we had second children of the opposite sex. I did – my second was a girl and, sure enough, I didn't have to buy any clothes for her for the first two or three years of her life. So, thank you Natasha for letting Eve borrow your clothes!"*
>
> *Maddy*

Borrowing or gifting – be clear

It is important, as with all arrangements involving friends, to be precise as to the terms you are agreeing to. Do you have a clear understanding as to whether you are borrowing these clothes or if they are being gifted? Mine were definitely only borrowed and, every six months or so, I'd return a big bag of clean outgrown items and swap them for the next size up.

Similarly, I have lent my son's clothes out to friends. Lending them has meant that his toddler clothes have gone on to clothe at least two other little boys, sometimes three.

KEEP SPECIAL MEMORIES JUST THAT – SPECIAL

Sometimes it might feel strange to watch another child running around in your child's extra special clothes. So, make up a bag of memories containing:

- A christening or naming ceremony outfit
- The coming-home-from-hospital kit
- The first pair of shoes
- The favourite jumper

These three or four items will be the ones you will cherish and perhaps only be willing to pass on if they are to grandchildren. So, keep them separate and be generous with the rest.

Once the day to day practicalities of childcare have been sorted out, there's the bigger issue of getting to grips with wider household finances to consider.

Cutting monthly outgoings

❝❝ There are two core problems with most families. Some are good at not overspending but have all the wrong products and throw literally thousands of pounds away through loyalty and inertia. Others overspend. They spend more than they earn, sometimes through a bizarre and very damaging sensibility that the more you spend the better a parent you are. Clearly that's wrong.

But by far the biggest financial waste is having the wrong products. **❞❞**

Martin Lewis, Money Saving Expert

For families sitting down and trying to deal with the enormous financial questions of whether to return to work, how to pay the bills, and whether childcare is affordable at all, it may not seem logical to address wider household bills first, but Money Saving Expert Martin Lewis believes it is essential. After all, if parents really are throwing thousands of pounds away each year through inertia or inappropriate customer loyalty, then simply by re-jigging their financial position they could dramatically change the monthly family budget.

However, before you instantly jump on the nearest comparison website and trade everything in for something new, from car insurance to bank accounts and phone tariffs, there are a few basics to get to grips with first.

KNOW WHO YOU ARE

Each financial relationship you have, whether it's with the cable company, the mobile phone company or the credit card company, is different. You regard these relationships differently, you use them differently, you even use them differently from other consumers who have the same accounts with the same providers.

That, above all else, should serve as a warning that there is no single product that will suit everyone. However, everyone can find the products that are best suited to their needs and their spending patterns.

Take the current account as a prime example. Despite being self-employed, I avoid going overdrawn at all costs. I might end up living on Clubcard vouchers and Boots Advantage points at the end of a month if no-one has paid me, but I'd rather do that then go even £1 overdrawn (a hangover from having been all too readily overdrawn as a student!). Other self-employed people cannot function in their business without an overdraft.

Overdrafts are hugely expensive, though not as much as they used to be, as many banks have overhauled their charges in light of the numerous court cases they've faced in the last few years. But finding the current account that either charges the least for overdraft users or pays the most for credit interest (depending on how you use it) could make a real difference.

So, it goes to show that you need to understand how you use each product BEFORE you shop around.

WHAT NEEDS REVIEWING?

Juggling work with two or more children and even determining whether that is financially possible is not something that families can come to gradually. Yet, examining every financial product within a family home does take time. Just by listing all the financial products that could do with a forensic review within your household, you can gain an understanding the enormity of the task ahead:

- Mortgage
- Current account
- Savings account
- ISA
- Credit card
- Home phone
- Internet connection
- TV/cable/satellite

- Mobile phone
- Gas
- Electricity
- Water
- Car insurance
- Home insurance
- Holiday insurance

Divide these into an order of priority. This matters because everything that requires a financial relationship of one sort or another (including the standing order to the satellite company) involves a credit check. So, change the important big ticket items first and leave the rest for later.

So, divide these items into three or four chunks; forensically examine all the options for each item in your first group before then changing to the best deal that suits your individual requirements. Then and only then should you move on to the second group.

Group One: the big ticket items

This is where most families can save the most money, which is why it's advisable to do it first.

Mortgage

This is the most expensive item and the one with the greatest potential savings. However, it's worth remembering though that the only way is up for base rates. This makes the question of whether to fix, go variable or plump for a tracker, more important than ever before. Some people can only deal with financial certainty and are prepared to pay more in the short term to do that. Others would rather have money now and gamble that rates won't rise too far. A key question to ask this year, when budgeting for your mortgage is: 'How high do rates need to rise before I'm stuck?' Answering this question might help you to decide whether or not to fix.

Current account

This is especially important if you either have a high residual balance each month or you go overdrawn. If you never EVER go overdrawn, then you could earn up to £100 a year simply by choosing the bank account that pays the highest credit interest. If you do sometimes go overdrawn, even if it's only by a fiver at the end of the month a couple of times a year, you need to find an account that charges you the least for using its overdraft facility. Different accounts suit different customers. The best place to go to for bank account advice (in fact, the oracle, as far as I'm concerned), as well as the consumer champion for excessive bank charges is Martin Lewis' website **www.moneysavingexpert.com.** Yes, there are other websites you can explore, but no other site gives such comprehensive information about *how* you should chose the best bank account to suit your needs and *which* type that will be once you've identified the sort of customer you are. What's more, the information is updated on his site regularly and it gives information on the various comparison sites, how they operate and what they are most suited for.

Savings account

There are plenty of internet-based savings accounts that offer much more competitive rates than traditional bank and building society savings accounts. Many are offered by big name institutions but on an internet-only basis. The questions to ask are: How often do you envisage needing to get access to your money? What are you saving for?

TOP TIP: DIFFERENT SAVINGS POTS FOR DIFFERENT NEEDS

If you are saving for a variety of different purposes then open a variety of savings accounts. That way you don't borrow from one pot to fund something else. It also means that money you can afford to keep locked away for longer could potentially earn more in interest.

ISAs

Savings and ISAs are not so much about cutting costs but about making your hard earned money work harder to give you greater returns. There is no reason NOT to have a cash ISA. By not using an ISA you are simply giving the tax office more of your money (not something many of us would volunteer to do under normal circumstances).

TOP TIP: GET ISA SAVVY

Many financial institutions try and lure savers in with good introductory or bonus rates that pay 1% or more above their usual rate for the first year. Whatever cash ISA you plump for, keep an eye on rates and, if you're not happy, transfer your ISA across to another provider. NEVER withdraw money from your ISA in order to transfer it – you'll immediately lose all the tax benefits. Instead, request an ISA transfer form from your new provider and they should sort everything out for you and keep your savings tax-free in the process.

Group Two: tarting and bundling

Frankly, that sounds rather rude. However 'tarting' refers to the act of constantly switching from 0% rate to 0% rate on credit cards. 'Bundling' refers to the way you can combine your cable/satellite, phone and broadband and possibly your mobile phone to boot, in order to make significant savings.

Credit card(s)

How many cards you should have and what type depends on how you use credit. For a full explanation, read the Money Saving Expert guide to credit cards at **www.moneysavingexpert.com/balancetransfers**.

To be a tart or not to be a tart:
£5,000 debt repaying £150 per month

		After 6 months		Until debt repaid		
Card	APR	Remaining Debt	Interest Cost	Time taken to repay	Total Interest	Saving
Standard Card: Smile	18.9%	£4,520	£420	46 months	£1,880	N/A
Bad Tart: 0% for 6 months	0% & 18.9%	£4,100	£0	42 months	£1,240	£640
Stable Relationship Transfer to Barclaycard	6.8%	£4,285	£205	37 months	£520	£1,360
Good Tart: Rotating 0% offers	0% + 3% fees	£4,100	£150	36 months	£270	£1,610

Note: Assumes cards are only used for balance transfers

(Source: www.moneysavingexpert.com)

As the table shows, over 6 months nothing beats 0% interest: it'll save a fortune. Yet over the longer time period, a stable relationship card beats everything but pure tarting.

Phone/cable/internet/mobile

How you choose to divide these up depends largely upon how you like to use these services and whether you wish to bundle (combine) any products together. Bundling can save hundreds of pounds.

Whether or not you want to bundle depends on where you live, what services you have and whether you can make significant savings by keeping them separate. It is possible, for example, to get line rental, broadband, free weekend calls and 6p/minute calls to mobiles for £16 a month *(source: www.moneysavingexpert.com)* without making further economies of scale, by adding a Sky or Virgin cable subscription deal into the package.

The first steps to consider are what you have and how you use it:

Cable/satellite

- Which channels do you watch the most?
- Which pay channels can you do without?
- Could you manage on a Freeview box, for example? If you cannot live without CBeebies but find you're not watching

Sky Sports as much as you used to then the answer might be 'yes'. If however, life would end without the ability to watch a live Premiership match each weekend then clearly a Sky/cable option is a must!

Home phone

- How often do you make calls?
- How long do these last?
- Do you work from home?
- Do you need to be able call overseas a great deal?
- Are many of your calls to mobiles?
- Are they daytime or evening/weekend calls?

Only when you've established a pattern of usage can you decide which deal will best suit your family and what you may need to consider within a bundling package.

TOP TIP: USE THE EXPERT

For more information, once again go to the oracle: **www.moneysavingexpert.com/phones**.

Group Three: utilities
Gas, electricity, water

At the moment, it is generally (but not always) cheaper to combine electricity and gas with an online dual fuel tariff than any other rate. And it is usually best to pay for utilities by monthly direct debit.

THE SIZE OF THE SAVING

For a London family who've never switched, are billed quarterly, and are annually spending £1,200 on gas and £900 on electricity, the cheapest equivalent service would save them £265 a year including cashback. If the family also started paying by direct debit then the saving would be £450, plus of course there's cashback.

Savings from switching

	Gas	Electricity	Total	Cashback	Total saving
Current – billed	£1,200	£900	£2,100	N/A	N/A
Switching to the cheapest					
Billed – Dual fuel	£1,895		£1,895	£30	£235
Billed – Standalones	£1,088	£777	£1,865	£30	£265
Direct Debit – Dual fuel	£1,694		£1,694	£30	£436
Direct Debit – Standalones	£1,036	£645	£1,681	£30	£449

(Source: www.moneysavingexpert.com)

Group Four: insurance

Insurances – home, car, holiday

For once, I am not going to suggest venturing on to Martin Lewis's website. Instead, insurances are what the comparison sites deal with the best, so it's best to go straight to them.

However, not all websites compare prices from the same providers; not all providers are listed (so companies such as Direct Line and Aviva have to be quoted for separately); and the small print of each insurance policy needs to be read carefully. This is why it is worth looking at information from more than one comparison site. Try **www.moneysupermarket.com**, **www.confused.com** and **www.gocompare.com**.

It is worth remembering that your efforts should be rewarded with significant savings, so it is worth the pain of a few hours trawling around the web.

HOW MUCH COVER ARE YOU GETTING FOR YOUR MONEY?

Look at the amount of the excess and the scope of coverage. With car insurance, look at whether you get a courtesy car during repairs; whether your choice of preferred mechanic is restricted; and whether you will be given a replacement child seat if your car has been damaged.

With home insurance, check what value of goods you have been insured for and whether you have to list high value items separately; whether you are insured for some of these items outside of the home (for example, wedding rings); and check whether or not you are covered for accidental damage. Some providers may charge more but they may also cover you for more too and therefore prove to be better value.

GET THE MONEY RIGHT AND THE REST BECOMES EASIER

It is a sad fact that more couples argue about money than anything else. There are hundreds of parents across Britain who have perfectly managed a career and a home before they had children, without ever once suffering a financial crisis. They could save up for a car, a holiday or the deposit on a house with reasonable ease.

Children change all of that in a heartbeat. Once they arrive, the basics of family economics – and squeezing every drop of value out of an increasingly insufficient pay packet – become the very cornerstone of a secure family life.

Secure doesn't mean rich. It means being able to live within your means. For the next two decades, that premise will be tested like never before. Therefore, get into the habit of reviewing your finances every year (or two). Crush the household bills down to size as much as possible and check periodically that your methods are still as cost effective as they can be.

8. Feeding your family

food and grocery shopping

Cutting weekly bills down to size

Little children may not add much to a weekly food shop, but by the time they are junior school age, their presence is certainly making itself felt in the family fridge.

There are ways of keeping a food bill low:

- □ Stick to water, not fruit juice
- □ Cut the booze bill down to size
- □ Avoid shop-bought snacks and make your own
- □ Go to different shops for different items
- □ Get gardening for summer salads and vegetables
- □ Don't do takeaways
- □ Avoid brand names

There is no more expensive way to do the weekly shop than to visit your local supermarket. They are designed to get you to spend, spend, spend. Their layout and even the way they pump the smell of freshly baked bread around the shop are designed to get you to part with more and more of your cash. Once you have understood that supermarkets are not there to provide everything for you in a convenient way but are there to fleece you of an ever increasing portion of your weekly earnings, you can adopt a different approach to shopping.

SHOP VIRTUALLY

If supermarkets are designed to get us to spend as much as possible, it follows that we will save money if we don't shop in them. Shopping online is a much cheaper alternative. You can still shop at the same store, still earn the same loyalty points and still benefit from the same special offers and BOGOF (buy one get one free) offers. You have simply removed the temptation to pick up a 'bargain' along the way.

 TOP DEAL

A rudimentary survey I completed (of mothers whom I researched for this book) suggested that, without changing brands or doing anything other than switching from store-based to online shopping. The average family saved at least £10 per shop.

Total savings: more than £500 a year
Those savings can be increased further by comparing prices across supermarket ranges.

SHOP AROUND

We are all busy people and, frankly, the idea of spending a day trekking from shop to shop just to get a bunch of bananas 20p cheaper somewhere else doesn't sound like the most effective use of time.

Luckily, **www.mysupermarket.com** can do that for us online. It looks at the cost of goods from four online supermarkets: Ocado, Sainsbury's, Tesco and Asda. For every item you wish to purchase it tells you which of those shops has the cheapest option. This can save families hundreds of pounds a year. The first time you use the system it takes a while to set up. However, you can save your shopping basket online, which makes subsequent shops far quicker and easier to accomplish.

DOWNGRADE YOUR SHOP

The reason why the supermarket chain Aldi can charge such low prices is that it doesn't stock hundreds of different varieties of each type of produce. Bananas are just bananas. There is one type of digestive biscuit available and one or two brands of tea bags. There are no 'basic' or 'finest' ranges. That way, stock is priced reasonably and shifts quickly.

So, to cut your food bill down to size, take a leaf out of the Aldi book. Don't opt for the 'finest' brand of everything, assuming it to be best. Try some basic ranges or own brand biscuits instead of McVities: take them home and see if you can taste the difference. If you are shopping online, **www.mysupermarket.com** has its own 'downshift challenge' section, which allows you to do the same online and see how much money you can save.

Money Saving Expert Martin Lewis is a key architect of downshifting and has examined this technique in detail both on his website and television. In his studies, most people only seemed to notice the difference in half the products that they downshifted. But changing these can make a dramatic difference.

TOP DEAL

For a family shop of £100 a week:
- Annual expenditure: £5,200
- Downshift everything: annual savings of £1,700
- Downshift only 'no-difference' items: annual savings of £800

Downshifting can cut 15% off a family's shop and save over £800 a year, without noticing the difference.

(Source: www.moneysavingexpert.com)

SHOP LOCALLY; SHOP SELECTIVELY

I buy different things from different shops where possible to cut costs. There is no Aldi or Lidl near me, which limits how I might use them, but I do have access to an Iceland. I buy staple goods such as breakfast cereal, milk, loo rolls, biscuits, yoghurt, and ice cream from here as it is significantly cheaper. I generally also find that buying fresh fruit and vegetables from the local greengrocer can save costs too. If you have a pound shop nearby, that could be a great place to stock up on washing powder, cleaning products, loo roll and other general household staples.

CHANGE YOUR ONE-STOP SHOP

Not everyone wants to shop around and constantly compare prices. For some, life is just too short to do that. If you want to cut your shopping bill down to size without changing your routine too much then simply change your shop. For example, Asda online can be cheaper than Tesco and Ocado because it tends to discount more lines each week. I can usually cut 10%–15% off my food bill by doing such a swap.

Grow your own

This is a longer-term strategy but one which is worthwhile for the whole family. Nonetheless, allotments take commitment and can be pricey. You will probably spend one afternoon a week up there in the winter and at least two afternoons a week in the summer, as well as evenings tending and watering. However, children love growing their own food and sampling the fruits of their labour.

The results are spectacular. Your family entertainment bill plummets because of the time you spend outdoors rearing crops and you get wholesome fresh produce. Little wonder, then, that many local councils have seen a surge in demand for allotments. As a result, some have started to offer half-sized plots and yet many still have waiting lists that last for years.

Once you and your family have got to grips with what you are good at growing (and what you're not!), you should find that the cost of the allotment, seeds, equipment and tools is easily covered by the savings you make in your weekly food bill during the summer months.

CROP-SWAP

Most successful growers end up with a surplus of one particular crop or another. If that happens to you, try and do a reciprocal deal with your fellow gardeners. You might find you grow the best rhubarb for miles around but cannot grow a raspberry if your life depended on it. Some gardeners have a knack for fruit, whereas others are great at lettuce and carrots. Grow what comes naturally and find a way to get that to work best for you. You'd be surprised just how much you can save.

> ❝ I've had my allotment since Louis was born. We've now got two. I don't have a big chest freezer – if I did we could be even more self-sufficient, but we do have a freezer and I do freeze a lot of stuff for the winter months. I'd say, over the course of the year, it costs me one month's food money per year to pay for the cost of the allotment and another month's food money for tools, seed, fertiliser and all that stuff. Out of that we produce enough food for about three weeks every month for around seven months of the year. What's more, it's a great outdoor hobby that gives us time together as a family. ❞
>
> Everton, dad of Louis

Everton's net savings add up to three months' food money each year, and those savings could be further enhanced by entering into a crop-swap with other committed growers.

GET THE MOST FROM SURPLUS STOCK

Most gardeners love the summer months, when there seems to be a bountiful harvest almost every week, even after the slugs have attacked the salad crop. If you have more ingredients than you know what to do with, try preserving some of your stock for the months ahead.

Frozen parsley cubes
Wash and drain parsley leaves. Finely chop the parsley and put into ice cube trays. Fill the trays with water and place them in the freezer. The frozen parsley cubes can then be taken out when needed to add to soup or sauce.

Home-made pesto
Pesto is a great way to use surplus basil. For every bunch of basil, which will need to be chopped finely, you will need a crushed clove of garlic and a couple of tablespoons of pine nuts, which also need crushing. Combine these together with olive oil (probably five tablespoons full), season to taste, and add 50g of finely grated parmesan cheese. Play with the combinations

until you have the perfect tasting pesto for your palate. Store your mixture in an old, cleaned jam jar with a screw-top lid in the fridge.

Home-made sun dried tomato

You don't need an allotment to grow tomatoes, just a sunny windowsill or two. And, if you are successful, you may well end up with more tomatoes than you know what to do with.

If you want to remove the skins first then plunge your tomatoes – a few at a time – into a pot of boiling water for a minute. Then scoop them out and place them straight into a bowl of iced water. This makes the skins really easy to peel off. Alternatively, skip that bit if you like your tomatoes still with skins intact. Cut them in half, cut out the tough part of the stem, cut in half again and remove the seeds if you have a particularly seedy variety of tomato. Then spread your tomato slices out on trays, sprinkle with seasoning: a couple of tablespoons of sugar and some olive oil. Then put them into the oven at its lowest setting (around 70°C–80°C) for around eight to 10 hours, then turn the oven off and leave the tomatoes to cool overnight. Transfer them to sealable freezer bags (leaving a little room for expansion) and freeze. They will last in the freezer for nine to 12 months and a bagful will last in the fridge for a month.

Freezing blackberries

As an avid blackberry picker, I have found the best way to preserve the fruits without them getting all mushy is to spread them out on baking trays when freezing to ensure they don't freeze as a solid mass. After they have been frozen, they can be scooped into bags and stored more effectively.

Freezing cooking apples

Cooking apples can be peeled, blanched and frozen in batches in freezer bags ready for use.

Storing eating apples

In the old days, the autumn harvest was stored over the winter perfectly successfully before fridges were invented. Eating apples are best stored wrapped individually in newspaper in a box or tea chest, with each layer covered in dried moss, grass or straw and kept in a cold dark place, like a garage, a shed or a loft.

Storing potatoes

When you first harvest potatoes you should leave them in the sun for a few hours to dry off and allow the skin to harden a little. Then brush off soil and check carefully for any damaged spuds. (Put these to one side and use them first.) Potatoes cannot be left in freezing conditions and cannot be exposed to light as they turn green, so they need to be stored in the dark: preferably in a hessian sack or in strong paper bags somewhere cool and dark (such as a garage). If you are storing in paper bags, leave the neck of the bag open to release any moisture. After you've been storing your potatoes for a month or so, wait for a fine day and empty out your bags. Re-check your crop for signs of rot or for any pesky slugs that evaded you first time around.

Storing root vegetables: carrots/parsnips/beetroot/celeriac/turnip/swede

Remove the foliage up to an inch above the crown. Place your crop in layers in boxes or crates, padded with a damp but not wet packing material (sand, coir, leafmould or peat are all good options). Keep your crop in a cold place (ideally between 0 and 4°C – colder than potatoes). If you can avoid doing so, don't place your crops in the loft as the temperature is too variable. A garage or allotment shed is probably best.

TOP TIP: YEAR-ROUND HOME PRODUCE

With some care and attention, you can store and therefore enjoy your home-grown produce all year round.

Plan meals and cook flexibly

A packet of minced beef isn't just good for one meal: it can double up as both a Bolognese sauce and a cottage pie. Even better, if you buy your minced beef on a BOGOF it could also work well in enchiladas and a chilli con carne while you're at it. Maybe you don't want to eat all those red meat meals in one week but that's why we have freezers!

If you can shop with half a mind on the evening meals you can create, you can examine the BOGOFs and the reduced items more effectively. The minced beef example is just that – an example of how you can use family recipes to maximise each fresh product you buy.

"I only ever buy fresh meat and fish in the reduced aisle. I can then either freeze it on the day or purchase or divide it into appropriate portions for different meals and then cook those and store them as required."

Maddy

GET MENU PLANNING

□ Porridge is filling and significantly cheaper than cereals.

□ Wholemeal bread fills you up for longer than white bread and yet it doesn't have to cost any more.

□ Packet sauces are an expensive way to cook.

□ Use leftovers to make delicious home-made soups.

□ Cutting out just one takeaway a week can add £100 a month to a family's food bill.

Working via a rotating menu system (on fortnight or four week cycle) ensures that you shop efficiently and cook efficiently. It also works well if you don't like cooking every day but want to spend one afternoon a week cooking four or five dishes that can then be warmed up over the coming days.

Dishes that are wholesome, filling and good value include:

□ Spaghetti Bolognese

□ Shepherd's pie

□ Cottage pie

□ Fisherman's pie

□ Cobbler

□ Soup

□ Crumble

□ Casserole

By using good menu planning and a combination of cheap ingredients and favourites, your food bill will be substantially cut down to size. (You can halve an average family's food bill by using a combination of methods listed here.)

CUT OUT FOOD WASTE

As a nation, we are focussing more on what we consume and what we waste. A government survey into our food waste has shown that the average family throws away £610 worth of food each year. Sadly 60% of this food has never been used or touched. It therefore makes sense to cut food bills down to size by cutting down food waste.

One way to do this is to get canny with leftovers.

- When fruit goes mushy and fruit salad is just too boring to contemplate (yet again) try some banana cake, caramelised pear tart or a mixed fruit crumble
- Bubble & squeak is still tasty
- Left-over mashed potato can be used with an egg to make great potato pancakes
- Left-over slivers of meat from a Sunday roast can be used in soups, casseroles or on pizzas.

Great economical ingredients

- Rice – both risotto and long grain rice
- Eggs –for omelettes, tortillas, cakes, potato pancakes, gnocchi, croquettes, bubble & squeak etc
- Pasta – virtually any leftovers can be turned into a sauce for pasta
- Flour – for all sweet and savoury cooking options (crumble, cake, pastry, batter)
- Sugar – caster and brown
- Butter
- Lentils – red ones can be used as filling and lose their shape more easily. Green ones need pre-soaking and stay firm (less easily disguised for fussy children!). They're great in casseroles and pies
- Pearl barley – a cheap and filling addition to soups and stews
- Stock cubes – both meat and vegetarian. Can be used for sauces and the base of soups
- Passata or tinned tomatoes – I'd be bereft without this staple in the cupboard

- □ Milk/cream/natural yoghurt – another cooking staple
- □ Cocoa powder

If your larder has these ingredients along with your family's favourite herbs and spices, you will be equipped to turn any leftover into a decent meal, or indeed to turn what you'd previously regard as one meal's ingredients into two separate dishes, with a little imagination.

> ❝ Carry water and children's snacks at all times. Get children used to drinking water from a very early age: they don't need fruit juice or fancy drinks. Also get children to eat porridge – it's very good for them and very cheap. ❞
>
> Claire, mum to Jack and Hamish

Feeding a family of four on £50 a week

There's nothing better than an example of economical food shopping – and what meals can be created from it – to give a flavour of just how this can be achieved for a family of four.

Netmums has shown it's possible to feed a family of four (two adults and two children) for less than £50 a week. Their total food bill came to £46 and main meals for a week cost £33. This is how they did it.

THE SHOPPING LIST

Fresh, frozen and chilled

- □ Chicken breast pieces
- □ White fish fillets
- □ Bacon
- □ Chicken wings/thighs/legs (depending on preference and price – buying a whole chicken is more economical than buying chicken portions)
- □ 625g cheddar cheese
- □ Two x 4pt semi skimmed milk
- □ Eight pork sausages
- □ Sunflower spread
- □ Two x six pack fromage frais
- □ Vanilla ice cream
- □ Frozen mixed veg
- □ Coleslaw

Dried goods

- ◻ 1kg rice
- ◻ Pizza base mix
- ◻ Cornflakes
- ◻ Porridge oats
- ◻ Variety pack biscuits
- ◻ 12 pack crisps
- ◻ Jelly
- ◻ 500g dried pasta

Tins, cartons and bottles

- ◻ Tin of sweetcorn
- ◻ Creamed tomatoes/passata
- ◻ Tomato puree
- ◻ Tin of red kidney beans
- ◻ Tin of green lentils
- ◻ Two tins of baked beans
- ◻ Tin of haricot beans
- ◻ Two tins of chopped tomatoes
- ◻ Two bottles of high juice squash
- ◻ Four one litre cartons of pure fruit juice
- ◻ One tin of tuna

Bakery

- ◻ One large baguette
- ◻ Two packs of eight crumpets
- ◻ Three sliced wholemeal or white loaves
- ◻ Two packs of six pitta breads
- ◻ Pack of 12 scones

Fresh fruit and vegetables

- ◻ Bag of mixed peppers
- ◻ Bag of onions
- ◻ Bag potatoes
- ◻ Broccoli (for fish pie)
- ◻ Two leeks
- ◻ Bag of carrots
- ◻ Garlic
- ◻ Bag of apples
- ◻ Basics bananas
- ◻ Basics pears
- ◻ Mushrooms
- ◻ Two lemons

THE MEALS

Breakfasts

Choose daily from:

- ◻ Cereal and milk
- ◻ Toast
- ◻ Porridge (with chopped or mashed banana)
- ◻ Crumpets and fruit juice

Lunches

Monday	Pitta bread with grated cheese and coleslaw, fromage frais and apple
Tuesday	Sandwiches, biscuits and pear
Wednesday	Sandwiches, fromage frais and banana
Thursday	Pitta bread with houmous, scones and apple
Friday	Sandwiches, fromage frais and banana
Saturday	Cheese and onion toasted sandwich, crisps and pear
Sunday	Leek and potato soup, crusty bread and scones

Main meals

Monday	Spanish rice
Tuesday	Pizza topped with peppers, onions and mushrooms, and left over chicken pasta salad
Wednesday	Veggie chilli with rice
Thursday	Baked potatoes topped with bacon, cheese and baked beans
Friday	Cowboy chicken and home-made potato wedges with mixed veg
Saturday	Sausage and bean hotpot with pasta
Sunday	Fish pie and carrots with jelly and ice cream for dessert

(Source: parenting website Netmums)

THE GOLDEN RULES OF BUDGET FOOD BUYING

- Avoid processed foods
- Cook from scratch – it's much cheaper
- Cut down on meat – use lentils and other pulses in your dishes
- Always try and use leftovers
- Avoid takeaways – make your own Chinese or curry: make lots and freeze some for later
- Bulk buy meat on offer and freeze the portion you don't need
- Shun fizzy drinks and juices in favour of squash and water
- Make your own cakes, biscuits, flapjacks etc
- Buy fruit and veg in season
- Root vegetables are great value

Get imaginative – try new combinations and explore recipes on websites such as Mumsnet and Money Saving Expert. Both have great forums where budget conscious parents swap ideas.

9. Going to school

Uniform

While going to school is a time for planning, it is also a time of unbridled joy – a rite of passage that you will look back upon with fondness. So, whether or not dropping your newly independent four or five year old off at the gates will bring tears to your eyes, it is a process to be relished. Nothing crystallises that process in the minds of parents and children alike than the purchasing of school uniform.

Many schools have their own logo'd sweatshirts that are available via the school shop (with funds going to the PTA) but in the vast majority of cases, most other pieces of uniform are generic and can be bought from supermarkets, school outlets or shops such as John Lewis and Marks & Spencer.

VALUE *AND* QUALITY

Being a parent who is reading this book, you will already be geared up to getting as much value out of your purchases as is possible. That should continue at school. Every June, July and August, the likes of Tesco, Asda and Sainsbury's compete to bring out the cheapest capsule uniform kit that it is possible to make and distribute. In 2009, Asda won this battle with a kit comprising polo shirt, trousers/skirt and jumper for £4. No doubt, by the time this book is on the shelves, that battle will be underway once more. However, as many parents know, price is not the same as value. Therefore, I have spoken to parents up and down the country for their views on which school uniform does what we need it to do: last, still look good, wash well without bobbling and survive whatever the little darlings decide to put it through.

Polo shirts/shirts

Wherever you buy them from, shirts tend to last better than polo shirts. That's not necessarily an ideal option for a four-year old who's not yet comfortable with buttons, but it is worth bearing in mind as your child(ren) get a bit older. Shirts stay whiter for longer; they can be soaked more easily to remove stains; and they are easier to iron. They also come in long-sleeved versions that work better in the winter. That aside, shirts don't suit every child and sometimes polo shirts are the only option. If that is the case, polo shirts from Marks & Spencer and Asda tend to keep their shape for longer.

Skirts

Again Marks & Spencer had many fans among parents, not least because the skirts washed well. Sainsbury's skirts also received favourable comments. Tesco skirts were criticised for getting too bobbly too quickly.

Pinafores

Marks & Spencer's recent style of pinafore dress that pulls over the head was criticised by a number of parents for being difficult to get in to. (Apparently the head hole was not generous enough.) That made getting changed for PE more of an arduous task than it needed to be. Pinafores from Sainsbury's, Tesco, Asda and John Lewis were all praised for being good value.

Trousers

John Lewis and Marks & Spencer were both praised for producing trousers that were that bit thicker and therefore less likely to knee too fast. Tesco trousers knee quickly and Sainsbury's trousers have discoloured around the knees quickly in some cases – particularly the grey ones.

Jumpers

John Lewis jumpers and cardigans wash and wear really well without bobbling. Second place goes to Marks & Spencer. In some cases the jumpers offered by supermarkets were criticised for fading too quickly, particularly the sweatshirt-type of jumper as opposed to the old-fashioned woollen ones.

Summer dresses

Sainsbury's dresses were praised for washing and wearing particularly well. By contrast, a number of parents mentioned that Tesco dresses had ripped round the seams before the end of a summer term.

 TOP DEAL

Judged on wearability and washability, Marks & Spencer was unanimously considered the best value outlet for school uniform by parents I spoke to for this book, particularly when using the three-for-two price promotion the store has run for the past couple of years. Clothes are more likely to be outgrown rather than outworn, which is a key criterion for any parent. The best value supermarket, based on parental feedback I received, is Sainsbury's.

GOING SECONDHAND

It seems odd to consider buying items secondhand when they are so cheap to buy new, but seasoned parents of school-age children know only too well the havoc that missing jumpers, odd sports socks and one trainer can play on the school run in the morning. When your gorgeous child has set off to school all clean and shiny in the morning, only to return four hours later tangled, bedraggled and stained with half their kit missing for the tenth time that term, you'll start to appreciate why secondhand uniform shops can be a good idea – even when a basic uniform is so cheap.

TOP TIP: START YOUR OWN SCHOOL SHOP

Don't have a secondhand shop? Start one up! My children's school didn't have a secondhand shop, so I started one. It takes me two or three days a term to organise and run and sells donated items of school uniform as well as kit for sports and hobbies; Brownies, Cubs, Scouts and Rainbows uniform; and coats. It raises between £100 and £200 a term for the school and parents get the chance to buy bits and bobs of kit without breaking the bank.

Top sellers:

- □ School jumpers – these are the most-lost items of uniform, so it makes sense that we sell more of these than anything else
- □ Football boots – invariably outgrown before they're worn-out
- □ Brownie/Cub kit
- □ Ballet uniform
- □ Coats

Least popular:

- □ Polo shirts – by the time we see them they're a little grey and mis-shapen!
- □ Shoes – people prefer to buy new shoes

Many parents won't buy secondhand clothes for their children, regarding it as shameful, perhaps, or inappropriate. However, with a greater emphasis on recycling than ever before, and a recession to survive to boot, there are more parents who are browsing and buying than usual. Those who do can get football boots for £3, top quality winter coats for £5, ballet and tap shoes for £3, wetsuits for £5 and crested school jumpers for £2.

> ❝ We ran a fashion show in school once or twice a year. Parents absolutely loved it as we got different children of all ages from across the school to take turns on the catwalk. All the clothes on show were from the uniform suppliers. We'd start with all the different uniform options and sports kit and then go on to fashion wear. Because of bulk orders, parents would get a discount if they ordered from the show (about 10%) and the school got 20% of the proceeds. It was phenomenally successful. ❞
>
> Kay, retired primary head teacher and Ofsted inspector

School meals

Ever since Jamie Oliver drew our attention to the Turkey Twizzlers being doled out at lunchtimes in schools across the land, huge efforts have been made by schools to produce a hot, nutritious, and balanced meal for pupils at lunchtime. For working parents who may not get home until late, this can provide a degree of peace of mind – knowing that their child is having something warming and nutritious during the day.

However, parents of fussy children may be concerned that their child will simply go hungry rather than eat something unfamiliar – clearly an unsatisfactory outcome if it continues for too long. Budget conscious parents will also know that, unless your child qualifies for free school meals, it is cheaper to provide a packed lunch than to pay the daily lunch charge at school.

FREE SCHOOL MEALS

Eligible parents have to apply for free school meals; they are not handed out automatically. They are the responsibility of the local council, so to see if you qualify, it is best to go via the local council website. Typically, children qualify for free school meals if the family is in receipt of any one of the following:

- Employment and Support Allowance
- Income Support
- Income-based Job Seekers Allowance
- The Guaranteed Credit element of the State Pension Credit
- The family is in receipt of the Child Tax Credit (not the Working Tax Credit) and their annual income does not exceed £16,040
- They receive support under part six of the Immigration & Asylum Act 1999.

Children of any family which receives Working Tax Credit will not be eligible for free school meals, regardless of the family's income. For those who do qualify, free school meals can provide a saving of around £10 per child per week – something that's definitely worth applying for.

PACKED LUNCHES

❝❝ Get children used to drinking water from an early age. It's free. Encourage your children to have packed lunch and use school clubs over outside clubs wherever possible – they're usually cheaper. ❞❞

Claire, mum to Jack and Hamish

School meals may be warm and more nutritious than before but they don't necessarily offer the best value lunchtime option for children. With the average school meal for primary school children costing around £2 a day, it makes economic sense for many parents to opt for packed lunches.

A typical lunch contains:
- A sandwich
- A drink (which is free if, like Claire, you train your children to drink water)
- A piece of fruit
- A yoghurt
- A cereal bar

The cost of this lunch will not usually exceed £1 a day, especially if you can put home-made flapjacks, brownies or banana cake in the lunch in lieu of shop-bought cereal bars. The upside is that you can halve the cost of your child's school lunch. The downside is that sandwiches can become repetitive and they don't provide a warming option during the winter months. To stave off sandwich boredom, try replacing a sandwich with a home-made pasta salad or sausage roll or, in the summer, vegetables and dips.

School clubs

Where clubs and interests are able to be pursued through school, they are invariably cheaper than when they are continued outside of school. In part this is because there are no overhead costs in addition to the cost of the skill itself (for example, venue hire and appropriate insurance), but it can also be because some clubs are run on a voluntary basis.

The local football league club in my region works in conjunction with primary schools to provide weekly football sessions for children in an after school club. It costs an average £15 per half term per child (£2.50 a session). Other football sessions for youngsters in the area cost between £5 and £6 a session: £30 per half term.

Similarly, music lessons in school tend to be cheaper. In part this is because they can be shared between two or three pupils, but also because peripatetic teachers can charge less in return for a slot in a named school that gives them greater certainty of income.

Most schools run choirs, drama clubs, chess clubs, netball, and football clubs. Some also hold music groups, orchestras and a wider range of sporting activities.

USING PARENT POWER

Schools with active Parent Teacher Associations (PTAs) can run a surprising array of clubs, which all contribute to the school's ethos.

> ❝ We had a very active PTA that really helped the school. We co-opted parents into the PTA and used their skills to help us run clubs in lunch times and after school. For example, we had a homework club that the parents ran on a rota system. It helped children of working parents get their homework done at a reasonable time in a supportive environment, but it also helped those who wouldn't otherwise have had the support they needed outside of school. I've also seen some great examples of parents who have clubbed together to purchase talent in the community and bring it into school where appropriate. ❞
>
> Kay, retired primary head teacher and Ofsted inspector

MULTI-TALENT SWAP-SHOPS

This is another little idea of mine that can be adapted and used in different formats, depending on how best it works within your own school community. Schools are huge vibrant communities but how much they are able to benefit their members (pupils, staff, parents and the school itself) depends upon how well each community pulls together and communicates.

It is easy to see, as parents, what we want for our children and what their needs are. It is often difficult to relate that to a wider community need, or even to want to view it in a broader context. However, if your child wants extra maths tuition they are unlikely to be alone. Other parents will be equally concerned about particular elements in their child's skills-set or indeed they might want to offer a hobby that is not available within the school's curriculum.

This is where a multi-talent swap shop can really come into its own.

What you do

The PTA, or a group of like-minded parents, find a venue where parents can post items (either online or on a notice-board somewhere at school). Basically, this is a bespoke system that you set up according to how you want it to work, but my suggestions would be that for every 'wanted' post that is put up, people have to accompany it with an 'offer' post.

WANTED VS OFFERED

Wanted: Maths tuition for Year 4 pupil
Offer: Babysitting once a fortnight or gardening help once a month

---

The reason this can work is that, no matter what skills parents have, there will be something they can offer. The aim is to get the hobby or help and support their child needs at zero cost. Many parents are time poor but are even poorer in resource terms. This way, they can find a practical way around the problem. In other words, we're harking back to the good old fashioned barter economy.

So, for example, a parent could put 'Wanted: violin lessons for seven year old beginner' and offer whatever they are able to in return. That offer could ether be a direct trade or a benefit to the school. For example, babysitting in return for lessons makes sense. But wider offers could be accepted: for example, DIY around school, gardening, or even helping to run a school magazine for Year 5 and 6 pupils. The possibilities are endless.

What will happen, of course, is that far more people will want individual-attention items than are prepared to offer individual tuition. However, the whole point of posting these items within a wider forum is so that the PTA is able to discern what trends there are in the needs of the school body moving forwards. Some of those needs might be able to be met through committed parental help; others will require skills to be brought into school from outside (something parents may be able to club together to achieve).

The real point – and joy – in this way of doing things, is to assess how the needs of the school body are changing over time and which parents may be able to help address those needs in the future.

No-one is time rich, not least parents. However, schools become greater the more parents volunteer to help. Even working parents can do their bit (perhaps by helping with gardening in the school grounds once a term). This system only works if a large proportion of parents (at least 20%) are willing to commit to something on a regular basis, but by doing so, every pupil and therefore every family can benefit.

Potential cost savings

Parents can save a fortune:

- ☐ Sports can traditionally cost from £60 a term
- ☐ Music lessons can cost £9–£25 a lesson
- ☐ Maths tuition can cost upwards of £5 a week
- ☐ Babysitters can cost as much as £8 an hour in some areas

Schools can save a fortune

If parents are willing and able to offer skills to a broad range of pupils, then schools can offer a wider variety of facilities for no extra cost. Given that schools are constantly battling with limited resources, this will appeal. Parent power can be used to run:

- ☐ Netball and football teams
- ☐ Homework clubs
- ☐ Maths clubs
- ☐ Art clubs
- ☐ Orchestras and choirs
- ☐ Drama clubs

That will enable schools to make more efficient use of the teaching resources they have. It will also make the school a vibrant community that other parents and children will want to become members of.

All it takes is 20%–25% of parents to become active members of the school community for this kind of system to work. For those looking to enrich the lives of their children for little or no cost, it is a logical course of action to take.

TOP TIP: GET CHECKED OUT

To save time and school resources and to be able to get your school community off to a flying start, apply to get a CRB (Criminal Records Bureau) check three months before you need it. Anyone who is helping with activities involving minors needs to undergo a criminal check, but these can take time to process, especially at the start of an academic year when there are lots of checks taking place.

Saving money away from school

Many of you will have made friends with local parents whose children are the same age, either because they live in the same street, because you've met up in the local playground, or through your antenatal classes. Many of you will be trying to balance work and childcare at the same time, so join forces.

1. **The turn–by–turn taxi.** Outside school activities are easier to manage if you know other parents and children at the same events. Save time (and petrol) by taking it in turns to ferry to and from various hobbies. Better still, if one of those hobbies is an out of school activity, take it in turns to collect the children from school, feed them tea and run them to the event. This will enable you to take turns to work later in the office and catch up on paperwork.

2. **The sleepover club.** This is a better option for junior-age children but those in Year 2 and upwards can still benefit from this option. Take it in turns on a Friday night to have other children over for a sleepover. It means that perhaps once a month you run a madhouse but, in return, you might get some quality time with your partner without spending a fortune on babysitters.

3. **The childcare rota.** If you are friends with other working parents, then why not join forces and take it in turns to pick the kids up from school and supervise homework? Just be careful how many children you involve in this process and how long you mind each other's children for each week. This is especially ideal for parents who work part-time. It may not cover all your childcare needs but it might enable you to afford to pay for appropriate childcare on

the remaining days, whilst giving your children the opportunity to socialise after school with their friends in a secure environment with parents you trust.

MAKING THE LAW CLEAR ON RECIPROCAL ARRANGEMENTS

Recently two detective constables were threatened with prosecution by Ofsted because their childcare swap arrangement was said to contravene the Childcare Act as it was a long-standing arrangement that lasted more than two hours a day. The government has intervened in this issue, and is due to pass legislation to clarify the Act to safeguard parents and prevent this type of situation arising again. So, you can enter into a regular childcare arrangement with another family without needing to be Ofsted inspected as a childminder, provided no money changes hands.

4. **Supergran.** Increasing numbers of parents are turning to their parents or parents-in-law to help bridge the childcare gap. A Skipton Building Society survey in 2007 said that 20% of mothers could only afford to return to work because of the free childcare support that their parents or in-laws were able to offer. This is not a purely British phenomenon: the Irish press have reported similar levels of grandparental help. For those thinking of seeking help from grandparents it is important to ask, not assume, and also to come to an agreement as to what is a reasonable level of support. More information on how to approach the issue of family help is outlined in Chapter 3.

❝ My parents and my mother-in-law help me out on alternate weeks. This means that they only do once a fortnight each, but the children get looked after by their grandparents in a stable routine two days a week while I go to work. I can concentrate on my job knowing that they can easily be picked up from school early should anything be wrong. The rest of the time I do childcare swaps with friends. ❞

Claire, mum to Jack and Hamish

AGREE TERMS OF BUSINESS WITH GRANDPARENTS FROM THE OUTSET

Some grandparents relish looking after their grandchildren; others believe it was hard enough work looking after their own kids, never mind someone else's.

1. Never assume grandparents will say 'yes' if you ask them to help out.
2. If they are willing to help, ask them what they would be comfortable doing.
3. Some grandparents will do this in lieu of occasional babysitting; others will be happy to babysit as well. Don't assume you can rely on grandparents for extras – always ask.
4. Find out how flexible the arrangements are. For example, if there is an emergency, will grandparents be willing to do a bit more or are they doing all they can manage?

Most grandparents are on a tight budget themselves, so it does no harm to find out what you can do to reciprocate. Examples might be:

• Buying the food shopping
• Paying for their annual holiday
• Paying their petrol and/or insuring/taxing their car

10. Peer group issues

Whether or not your child has grown up surrounded by other children, once your child is firmly established in primary school the peer group issues will start. Some of these are relatively small scale and easy to negotiate. From which is the preferred brand of football boots to where swimming badges should be sewn to fit in with friends, you will be bombarded with a myriad of little peer group issues every day.

> *"Even the smallest issue can be a big deal to a primary school child. My daughter had a bee in her bonnet because she was the ONLY child in her ENTIRE year not to be given cheese strings in her lunch box. Honestly. You'd think there were more important things in life. Apparently not to a six year old."*
>
> *Maddy*

All of these issues are reasonably easy to deal with. Adidas Predator boots may be the boots of choice but they don't suit every shape of foot and not every child in the school will own a pair.

Similarly, no child needs a new football shirt each season (at £30 a pop). Some boys might collect them in the same way most boys collect Match Attack cards but therein lies life's toughest lesson.

Needing to fit in

Even in the early years of primary school, nagging parents for the next must-have toy isn't really about the toy. It's about needing to fit in. This only escalates during adolescence and can cause friction between parent and child. If your child is the odd one out in material terms then, like it or lump it, this can become a root cause or trigger for bullying.

For parents already struggling to make ends meet this is hardly the good news story you wanted to hear. However, it does go to show how important it is for parents to pick their battles wisely; to give in on less important issues so that they can be clear on the really big issues.

COMMON BATTLEGROUNDS

Many of these will be dealt with in detail later in this chapter but let's look at a number of the battlegrounds you will face in the years to come:

- □ **Birthday parties** – how many children to invite and what 'theme' or super-catered venue to choose.
- □ **Christmas** – will your child be the ONLY one never to have visited Santa in Lapland? I sincerely hope not, for your sake!
- □ **Pocket money** – such a contentious issue that there is a whole chapter devoted to the subject (see Chapter 11).
- □ **Hobbies** – even if you think your child has an ideal balance of interests they will fight over them.
- □ **Clothes** – from what brand of wellies and which coat they have; to not wearing skirts or only wearing skirts; to certain makes of trainers; it's all there, ready to be fought over.

SETTING GENERAL FAMILY RULES

Disagreement is only natural. After all, if you are a parent you are there to be the great big dragon figure that is soooooo unreasonable. If you've not heard the phrase, 'It's not fair' at least 10 times before your child reaches the age of seven, either your child is an angel or you are!

There are strong financial reasons for setting family rules. When your child reaches adolescence, the battlegrounds become more serious. If your child has known all along that there are sound reasons behind your judgement it should (in theory) help you negotiate these bigger battles.

Most importantly of all, however, the reason you set rules now, when your child is in primary school, is to enable them to learn over the next decade when it is reasonable to follow the crowd and when it isn't. There are too many adults in Britain today with serious debt issues. Many of those debts have been run up on credit and store cards. While there are some tragic stories of unfortunate circumstances behind some of those tales, many have spent their way to the brink of bankruptcy by failing to work to budgets and simply spending more than they earn over a period of years.

Learning to budget, develop sensible spending patterns and separate 'wants' from 'needs' is a complex job many adults (myself included) fail to achieve much of the time. When you're young and childless, this can be less of an issue. With children around there is less financial room for manoeuvre, and your spending patterns and financial attitudes can be subconsciously adopted by children.

Teaching children to live within their means is a hard lesson – probably one of the hardest lessons to learn. Essentially, it means teaching children to say 'no' sometimes to things they really, really want. It also means teaching them to wait or to choose one much-aspired-to item over another.

TOP TIP: BE CONSISTENT

Whether you are a single parent, married, co-habit, whether you have married a subsequent partner, whether you foster, adopt or have your own birth children it doesn't matter. The rule is the same: be consistent. Children are manipulative and can spot a crack in your wall of argument. If one parent says 'no' and they believe the other will say 'yes', they will lie about asking one and go and seek the views of the other. Even if you don't get on with your ex, this is an area where you will have to try and make common cause for the sake of your child.

So, regardless of where you draw the battle lines, you have to:

1. **Be consistent.**
2. **Speak with one voice**. If that means you say, 'I don't know. Wait until I've spoken to your mother/father', so be it. There aren't that many decisions that have to be taken straight away. Even if you have to make an instant decision and are uncomfortable doing so, email/text or phone the other relevant adults and explain what decision you have taken and why. They may not like it, but they need to know your reasons so they can support the decision.
3. **Never criticise your partner's decision or choice in front of the children.** They may have been a prize nincompoop, but that's for you to discuss with them out of earshot of the kids. You might have to discuss how to change the decision but do it together and make sure it is done away from flapping ears.
4. **Don't contradict or undo a decision already taken by your partner or the other parent.** This is especially hard for estranged parents who might find any dealings with the other party difficult. However, unless you avoid contradicting your partner's decisions, the battleground will shift away from the issue and back to the familiar old war of attrition between the two of you as parents. Your child will know this and use it, with increasing effectiveness over the years.

Waiting

One of the issues you'll quickly come to deal with is just when is it OK for your child to have something immediately, and when is it acceptable for them to wait? Every family has different rules for dealing with this. My husband and I have worked out a set of parameters through negotiation that generally work for our family. Roughly speaking they are:

□ If it is needed for school, it's OK immediately.
□ If something has been lost (we have a very absent minded child), a replacement has to be earned through chores or through making an effort to be organised for a prolonged period.
□ Most other things can wait.

Of course, our attitude to this issue doesn't always gel with other members of the family. Plenty of the parents who gave me feedback for this book talked of their frustrations when they had told their child to wait for a longed-for item only to find granny had jumped in and 'helped out'. What is family, if not a source of friction?

In most families, the benefits that contact with a loving grandparent brings far outweigh the irritation factor when grandparents indulge. In some ways, that is their job and it can help, rather than hinder parents in defining their own role. However, if occasional indulgences turn into something more frequent or threaten to overwhelm a delicate financial or emotional balancing act, talk to that family member and see whether there is an arrangement you can come to, as adults, that suits everyone.

This brings me neatly on to the final two golden rules for this chapter.

5.   **At some point, your child will be out of step with their peer group**. If not, you are not doing your job properly.
6.   **You are the parent.** Not the indulgent aunt/uncle.

Birthday parties

The children's party scene has now become a professional war zone. Just Google 'children's parties' and you will come across page after page of companies, dedicated to providing the 'perfect' experience for your child, all for a few hundred pounds. What's more, that's not the end of the spend. Oh no. There are party bags (and if you think kids don't notice which party provided the best bags, you're very much mistaken), there's the venue and there's the food.

Now, when I was little, my mum did parties for me and about 10 of my friends at home. There's a grainy photo of me aged three, having a party feast on the floor in my house. Parties were small, manageable and what's more, they were done at home in an affordable way. Pass the parcel had one winner. There were no sweeties between each layer of newspaper. The games were there to be played for their own enjoyment, not for the prizes, and we all ate pink wafer biscuits and jam sandwiches and then went home.

To show my age, that was the 1970s, not the 2010s, but there are still ways to give your child a memorable party without it breaking the bank.

1. **Don't feel you have to throw an enormous party before your child is at pre-school.** For the first three years (or as long as you can), your child will enjoy having a family get together with balloons and cake. That's all they need to know they are wanted, loved and you have all remembered their day.

2. **Find a friend.** Shared parties are fantastic because parents share the organisation, planning and excitement of the event, as well as the cost. My son's birthday was one day after one of his friends. They're in the same football team and were in the same class so they were always going to invite many of the same people. It made sense for us to share the party burden.

3. **Keep the numbers small.** Tempting as it is to invite everyone in the whole class to your child's party, be realistic. Your child is never going to be best friends with 30 other children. A dozen kids are more than enough to cause havoc!

4. **DIY.** My two children have been to many parties over the years, yet the ones they remember were often the simplest. Look at the suggestions below and see how you could vary these to suit your child.

5. **Opt for outings rather than parties in junior school.** Once children are older, they are pretty set in their friendship groups. So, instead of an enormous party, why not take your child plus three friends to the cinema. The older they get, the greater the variety of things you can do with them to make a memorable day.

Remember, your child's party is about building happy memories. If you are worried about the cost or scale of a party, your child will pick up on those worries and the emotion of deep unease will be the dominant factor of the day. So, stick to what you can manage. After all, dealing with lots of other kids is going to be stressful enough, without adding unnecessary financial pressure into the mix.

PROFESSIONAL PARTIES

Kids can have anything from bouncy castles (if your garden is big enough), to fairy entertainers, magicians, football coaching parties, swimming parties, pirate parties, even animal handling parties. Costs vary depending on whereabouts in the country you are. However, the following costs are intended as a rough guide.

Sports parties
Local authority leisure facilities can arrange multi-sports parties, either indoors or outdoors. They cost more if you want trampolining included as one of the activities. **Cost: £90–£150**

Swimming party
These can often be done with loads of pool inflatables at the local leisure centre. **Cost: £100–£150**

Magicians
Magicians can be hired for one to two hours. They can bring their own prizes for the kids and various entertainment options, including bubble machines for discos and disco lights. **Cost: £100–£250**

Bouncy castles
If the hired hall or back garden is big enough, a bouncy castle can be a great way to allow children to let off some steam. **Cost £100–£300**

Football coaching party
These are often charged on a per-child basis and are subject to a minimum number of children. **Cost: £7–£12 per child**

Bowling/Laser Quest
Bowling and Laser Quest parties come into their own when children reach junior school age because they offer lots of excitement. However they don't come cheap. **Cost: from £10 per child**

Many of these parties may need parents to incur additional costs such as party food, and sometimes even venue hire. Here are some ways to cut those costs down to size.

THE HOME-MADE PARTY
Generally speaking, a bevy of boys in your home is more stressful than a bunch of girls, but either can be better managed if there is something definite for them to do. Here are some suggestions and what ages they might suit.

The puzzle party

Suits: junior age boys or girls

Divide your party guests into teams and establish a set of puzzles. These can be old fashioned brain teasers or building tasks with Lego: whatever your toy cupboard and your imagination can muster.

Pit teams against each other or against the clock on a set of challenges. You can make the challenges as easy or as hard as you like. It will exercise the brain cells and be frenzied and exciting without turning into a riot.

The arty crafty party

Suits: infant age girls

Girls are generally happy to muck around with glue, glitter and paint until the cows come home. There are now so many craft kits that it's easy to have a party based around an art activity. Here are two examples given to me by mums.

 Erin had 12 girls at her party, including her. Each had a plain white T-shirt with their name and the date of the party on the bottom for them to decorate with fabric paints during the party. They then got to take that home as their going home present. 〃

Andra, mum to Erin

ⓔ TOP DEAL

Erin's party was organised by Arty Tots but you could do it yourself.

- T-shirts from **www.buytshirtsonline.co.uk** cost £1.80 each.
- Fabric paint costs £6.99 for a pack of 12 brush-on paints from **www.wardoliver. co.uk**.
- **www.amazon.co.uk** has sets from £4.16 for 8 fabric pen colours.
- A similar alternative would be to get plain cotton duffle bags from **www.fabric–paint.co.uk**. They cost just £1.67 each for 10 or more.

Total cost: under £30

❝❝ We got some cheap plain wooden photo frames for Ella and her friends to decorate, and got a load of glitter, glue, glitter pens and paint for them to design on the frame. Then, while the girls were having their birthday tea, we took a photo of all the children, printed out a copy for each of them and popped it in their frame as a going home present. It worked really well. ❞❞

Lindsay, mum to Ella

TOP DEAL

- Lindsay got her frames from Wilkinsons. They cost £1 for a pack of 3.
- Paint, stickers and glitter pens cost £10.

Total cost for 12 children: £14

THE OUTDOOR PARTY

Sadly, the outdoor party relies on something we just cannot take for granted: the weather. Therefore, it is always good to beg or borrow plenty of gazebos before pitching up in the local park.

Football party

Suits: junior age boys and sporty girls

Boys and girls can play football: just make sure the teams are divided by a grown up, not chosen by the children – otherwise you run the risk that the entire school footy team will congregate on one side and beat the other team 15-0. Mix abilities, ages and genders among the teams. Liven things up with:

- A crossbar challenge: five points for each player who can hit the crossbar from the penalty spot.
- A shoot off: each team lines up in turn to see which can shoot the most penalties. Add more and more goalies for extra fun.
- Crab football: as you can imagine, you have to sit on all fours to play this game.

A games party

Suits: girls and boys of all ages

This party could suit any group of children of any age. It also means you can choose the games to suit your venue and the ages. Suggestions might include:

- Softball
- French cricket
- Team hide-and-seek
- Obstacle races
- British bulldog
- Three-legged/ piggy back/wheelbarrow races – just be careful of injuries!

Young children in particular might enjoy bringing a teddy with them for their own Teddy Bears' Picnic after the games are done.

PARTY BAGS

These days, party bags are not an optional extra: they are a requirement. However, the contents of a party bag can, if you're not careful, add up to more than the party itself. Bags full of plastic blow-outs, whistles, a pencil and a slice of cake can add as much as £5 a head on to your party bill. The average cost per bag (based on parents I've surveyed) is between £2.50 and £3. So, if you've invited half a class full of kids and given each of them a party bag you could have spent around £40. Here are some ways to cut those costs down to size, assuming the party has 15 guests.

Dispense with bags

The 'themed' bags are only there as receptacles for birthday cake. So why not just hand out your going home souvenir and cake instead? Alternatively, use greengrocer's paper bags or wrap a souvenir up in newspaper and tie it with a ribbon. **Average cost saving: £5**

Buy pre-filled bags

For those who still want to hand out traditional party bags, opt for pre-filled ones that cost 99p each from websites such as **www.monsterparties.co.uk**. **Cost saving: £27.65**

Give a book as a take-home gift

Many parents of infant children have, quite rightly, become huge fans of
The Book People (**www.thebookpeople.com**). They buy packs of 10 books
for £10 and hand those out instead of plastic toys. They last longer and they
can choose the types of books that will suit the age and gender of the party
guests. **Cost saving: £27.50**

Give a souvenir of the day

With Andra and Lindsay's party ideas (above), the going home present was
part and parcel of the party itself. If you've got a smaller group of older
children and you've taken them on an outing, think ahead of something
small and simple that will remind them of the day. For example, Amazon.
co.uk sells magnetic photo printer paper for £1.55, for a pack containing
two sheets. So, you could get a photo of your group of kids, print a copy out
for each child and they get a fridge magnet picture to remind them. **Cost
saving: £30**

> My niece had 14 friends to a party recently. They each got a
> party bag with a slice of cake and a handful of sweets from a
> multipack and they couldn't have been happier – and it cost
> very little. Same for my nephew's second birthday party.
>
> Sally, aunt to Lauryn and Fergus

Toys and gadgets

GAMES CONSOLES

As children get older, some of their games can become more expensive. The
ones that seem to cause the most envy among children, and therefore the
biggest headaches for parents, are the gadgets. Sooner or later, you will face
a battle over:

- A Nintendo DS Lite
- A Wii
- A PlayStation
- An Xbox
- A PSP

It doesn't end there. Some of the best games cost between £25 and £40 each and, with the Wii, there is an endless array of new mats, steering wheels, paddles and other 'essential' equipment that your child will view as must-have for the games to function at their best, and you will view as an unmitigated rip-off. For each electronic toy, the fundamental questions remain the same:

- □ What is an appropriate age to buy this item?
- □ Will it be played with?
- □ Does it fit in with our family life?

Some children have DS Lites when they are aged five or younger. Others have to wait until they are seven or eight. With anything high value and electronic, the issue is not what age do all the friends acquire such toys, but rather what age do you, as parents, think is an appropriate age for your child to be given this item.

DS Lites are great. Children can entertain themselves on long journeys, at the end of a very dull extended family meal while the grown-ups are still talking, and other such occasions. However, they may also, unless limited, turn your bright and chatty child into a monosyllabic grunter who only responds to a little luminous screen.

For your child, gadgets will not be either/or options. Children will see nothing wrong in asking for a PSP when they already have a DS Lite, or requesting an X-Box as well as a PlayStation. They don't see that these machines are produced by rival companies competing in the same space. So, don't yield, simply explain.

I LIKE USING THIS ANALOGY:

'Wanting two consoles would be like daddy supporting two football clubs: Manchester United and Manchester City ... and that's not going to happen in a month of Sundays!'

So, in the same way that dad stayed loyal to the club he chose as a boy, your child will have to choose a console. With the cost of games and the cost of a console they're going to be stuck with that choice.

In this way there is a great deal of advantage to be gained in being the last family to yield to computer games. You can find out from the practical examples of parents around you:

- □ Which gadget has proved to be the best value
- □ Which is played with the most
- □ Which is the most sociable for the family
- □ Which is the most user-friendly
- □ Which is the easiest to buy new games for
- □ How many games are realistically played with
- □ Will it simply become another battleground you can do without or can it be used as a source of bribery for homework/chores/good behaviour?

If you delay buying games for as long as you can your child will not lose out: he or she will simply play with their friends' games on play dates instead!

MOBILE PHONES

While you will come across children in the primary school playground that have been given mobile phones at a very early age, there is little to justify children having a mobile phone before they start taking themselves to and from school. At the moment, half of five to nine-year-olds own a mobile phone (source: www.supernanny.co.uk). My first reaction, as a Luddite, is to ask, 'Why? Most of these children aren't taking themselves to and from school: there is no safety reason why they should have a phone, therefore it is an expensive status symbol.' However, that argument disappears when children reach the top year of primary school (Year 6) and are generally allowed to travel independently to and from school.

Secondary school, on the other hand, is a whole different kettle of fish. Your child will have progressed from a relatively small environment where all the teachers knew him or her by name and the journey to and from school was reasonably quick, to an enormous school that encompasses children from a variety of primary schools in the area. Few teachers will have a handle on all the pupils' names, your child has to travel further each way and will have to take themselves off to clubs and activities on a variety of public transport after school, which may or may not be reliable.

Whenever you take the plunge, mobile phones bring with them a whole array of issues you and your child need to be aware of.

Your child might be a victim of theft

Levels of street crime committed against teenagers are on the increase, primarily because they are flashing their gadgets about. Whether it's an iPhone or not, you need to tell your child to keep their phone out of sight as much as possible.

Beware of the cost

Even if you decide that your child does warrant a phone, it is probably better to get a pay-as-you-go mobile for your child. If they run out of credit, you can still contact them. At the same time, they cannot run up huge debts on your mobile phone bill with a pay-in-advance facility like this.

> ❝ My sister-in-law allows my niece £10 a month and if she spends that then she just has to wait for the next month. Any fuss, grumbles etc and she knows the phone will be taken from her. It's also a good way of letting children learn to budget and think about how they are spending money. ❞
>
> Sally, aunt to Lauryn and Fergus

> ❝ When I purchased a mobile phone for my son a few years ago, I thought it was the perfect vehicle for helping me stay in contact with him. I was certain I could afford the basic monthly charge ... but I never considered the exorbitant amount of time he would spend on the phone with friends. The monthly bill was continuously three times the amount I'd anticipated. Yes, the phone did allow me to keep tabs on my son when I wanted to talk to him or know where he was, but it also meant he instantly knew where everything was happening in and around where we live. The mobile has made his social life much easier to co-ordinate – which, in itself, increased his running costs! ❞
>
> Phil Clavel, Supernanny expert

Phil cancelled the contract. His son lived without a mobile for a year or two and now pays for his own mobile. His mantra is: 'Thou shalt not sign mobile phone contracts for thy teen'.

Beware hidden costs

Kids love downloading different ringtone services, logo screensavers and any gizmo going that looks cool. Sadly, these have a cool price tag that your child may not be aware of. If your child is on pay-as-you-go, they could blow all their credits on a single icon without realising. Make them aware that many of these 'services' have regular charges, not one-off payments. If you have put them on your phone tariff, keep a close eye on your bill for unusual charges. Also, most smart phones these days are multimedia devices, so beware of inappropriate website access and data charges. It is best to contact the network provider and register the phone as belonging to a child: that should ensure your child cannot access unsuitable internet sites or rack up expensive fees.

Premium phone numbers

Children can be extremely money-savvy if they are told what to look out for. You could get premium number calling blocked on your child's phone. Alternatively, you could explain to your child which numbers cost more and let them learn – especially if they are paying the bill! Either way, they need to be aware what a premium number is, how much it costs and what impact just one call a day at that rate could have on their pocket.

The best place to go for more information is **www.phonebrain.org.uk**. It was set up by PhonepayPlus, the UK regulator for phone-paid services to educate young people about phone services – and the costs they incur!

Christmas

Christmas is just more Christmassy with children around. However, that can mean that costs escalate, as it becomes more of a production and less of a religious celebration.

> ## HOW MUCH DOES CHRISTMAS COST?
> - Asda: The Cost of Christmas survey, compiled by Asda in 2009, showed the average UK household would spend £399 on food and presents in November and December 2009, compared to £413 in 2008.
> - Moneyhighstreet.com: £665 on average per family. It is estimated that we spend £410 on presents, £170 on food and £85 on travel.
> - Principality Building Society: average spend in Wales was £784.

It seems how much we spend depends on who you ask, but we could always spend less.

No-one wants to be a complete humbug and ban Christmas. It is an important occasion that instils important sentiments of family, charity and collective giving. The danger, with children, is that by hitting the shops in a spending frenzy, we are showing our children that mad-dash consumerism is something which should be accomplished at this time of year.

KEEP COSTS DOWN
To keep costs to a minimum, and to pass on the best messages of Christmas without taking all the fun from the occasion, here are some suggestions for keeping festive costs down.

Buy wrapping paper, crackers and other storable items in January
The minute Christmas is over, the stores discount their seasonal items. So that is precisely the time canny shoppers head out and stock up ready for the following Christmas. It is not unusual to get rolls of paper for a quarter of their original price.

Keep spending where you can see it
If you like shopping virtually, then write down everything you have spent, including the cost of packaging and postage per item, to make sure you've got a true idea of your spend. Before you spend anything, always compare prices using one of the many price comparison sites like Shopzilla or Kelkoo. And, while it's nice to know that the likes of Amazon will gift wrap your present, it still comes in a cardboard box so is it really worth an extra £3?

Set a limit per person before you shop

Change 'What can I get him/her', to 'What can I AFFORD to get him/her?' Shopping is psychological warfare. Retailers use all manner of extremely sophisticated techniques to get us to spend more with them. So, beat them at their own game. Before you even consider what to buy for someone, set a limit and then choose a present to fit that limit.

Combine presents and cards

Purchase a charity present online and the 'gift' will be sent to the recipient as just a simple card. Oxfam Unwrapped, for example, allows you to buy gift donations for needy groups abroad on behalf of your friends and family. Buy a cow, seeds, new school books, vaccinations, or even an entire classroom for each of those family members you won't be seeing this year to exchange presents with, and save not only on a separate present and card, but also the postage. Plus, you get to help needy groups around the world and beat consumerism at its own game.

Make your own

The Christmas card list gets longer each year – and so does January's recycling mountain. A family of four can spend nearly £40 on Christmas cards. Why not either make a one-off charitable donation in lieu of cards or make your own? Kids love getting creative at Christmas and by using a simple print or wrapping paper motif you can create something unique. Save on wrapping paper too by using old wallpaper, or newspaper bound with a tinsel bow.

Kids also love getting creative and making presents. Suggestions could be:

- □ Foodie gifts such as cakes, cookies, or home-made mincemeat are great.
- □ If you have a fruit tree or you like foraging for blackberries etc, then you could make loads of jams and chutneys as presents.
- □ Autumn term is the time for school photos. Most grandparents, aunts and uncles like one of these, so turn it into a present by buying and decorating a simple wooden picture frame.
- □ Get knitting – if your skills don't stretch to a jumper, they might stretch to a funky scarf!

- □ Make dolls for kids – home-made dolls are fantastic and can come in all shapes and sizes, from wooden spoon dolls to rag dolls.
- □ Accessorise or upgrade an existing toy as a present.

"My daughter has a dolls house from the Early Learning Centre. One year, for a present, I painted it. It is now pale pink with stone mullioned windows, a black front door, and terracotta chimney pots. My son helped by painting the kitchen stove with silver enamel paint, and my mum joined in by finding and buying the flooring and wallpaper for us to decorate the interior. It took a great deal of time and a lot of love but was a fantastic gift idea and now her dolls house is bespoke."

Maddy

If all else fails, give a present of your time

Draw up some home-made vouchers to pop into envelopes that will suit the recipient. They could be for gardening, babysitting, ironing etc. The point is that they are given with thought and love.

CHRISTMAS FAMILY AGREEMENTS

Sometimes we start out with all the best intentions, but they are then undermined by well-meaning relatives trying to get something special 'just to see their little faces when they open it'.

You know you've heard that phrase!

The best way through is to chat to family members and see if you can agree a way forward. Three of the most successful suggestions that came in from mothers I interviewed were:

Setting financial limits

Everyone agrees that, no matter who they are buying a present for, that person's gift will not exceed a set amount. You can set the limit at whatever you like depending on the size of your family, but, once it's agreed, you can relax, knowing that you no longer feel compelled to make a significant financial gesture with your present.

Do a family secret Santa

This works very well in families where everyone gets on. Everyone can name ONE item (within reason – no sports cars!) they really want for Christmas. Children are included in the list at this stage. Then the children's wishes are divided among the adults and the adults also each choose ONE adult to buy for at random. Everyone gets something great, without it turning into a present frenzy.

The charity Christmas

You can only buy gifts secondhand or from charity shops. This makes present buying more interesting because the purchaser has to search really hard to find something that will suit its recipient. This is a great idea on many levels. The charity benefits, you are promoting recycling and therefore spending in a responsible way, and you have to spend time and choose carefully so the gift automatically comes with love. Finally, the charity shop Christmas means that every gift has the potential to be quirky.

TOP TIP: STAY IN BUDGET

Only spend what you can afford at Christmas. The best Christmas present is the one given with thought, not the one given with debt.

PLANNING FOR CHRISTMAS

It is always a good idea to set money aside each month for Christmas into a separate savings account. You can use any account for this: it doesn't have to be a specific Christmas club or supermarket Christmas stamp scheme.

> *"My council tax bill is only paid monthly for 10 months of the year. During the two months when I don't pay council tax, I siphon off the money I would have used into a savings account. That is my Christmas pot."*
>
> *Maddy*

❝❝ As well as putting an amount in a savings account each month, I save up any two-pound coins I receive. Over the course of a year they probably amount to about £250 or so, which I then use at Christmas to pay for something special. ❞❞

Roger, dad to Chris and James

THINGS TO AVOID

Father Christmas should not bring big presents

Parents create a rod for their own backs if Father Christmas can magic marvellous presents out of thin air, such as bicycles or TVs. It can easily be explained why Father Christmas just cannot do that: after all he has all the children in the world to look after. All he brings is a token of joy and love to good little boys and girls everywhere. That means, of course, that when little boys and girls realise that you-know-who is a myth, there is no enlightened self interest in perpetuating that myth.

Lapland is an expensive marketing opportunity

Yes, thousands of children a year do visit Lapland at exorbitant cost for the thrill of meeting the 'real' Father Christmas. Why? Doing so only destroys the Father Christmas that your child has nurtured in their imagination since they became aware of Christmas. Let them keep their Father Christmas dreams.

Real trees

An artificial tree will cost the same as a real one the year that you buy it. However, thereafter, it is free, saving you around £50 a year. Yes, I know it's unsentimental but it is also economic good sense, it doesn't drop needles all over the house, and you don't have to wonder how on earth you're going to strap it to the roof rack to get it home.

School trips

There are school trips and then there are school trips. For the majority of the time, this is not really an issue in primary school. The really big trips – such as sports tours aboard, skiing trips, geography field trips to far flung corners of the world – tend to come thick and fast in secondary school.

In some ways, it's a good thing if your child gets invitations to more than one trip in any school year – it means that:

- □ The school are proactive in encouraging the children to gain greater experiences.
- □ The staff are ready and willing to supervise children on a variety of trips, which means there is a lot going on and your

child can benefit from this buzz of excitement and thirst for knowledge.

□ It could also mean that your child is doing particularly well as some of these trips are only for a select few pupils (such as sports tours).

This is great, but expensive.

School trips have evolved. Not all schools offer a ski trip to the Alps by coach. Many now fly to places such as Whistler in Canada because they can guarantee the snow. That's all well and good but it puts the cost of a ski trip up from around £800 per pupil to £1,600 for a week.

Then there are geography trips. While it was fine for us to look at the effect of the ice age on the topography of North Wales or examine the Jurassic coastline of Dorset and Devon, these days, pupils examine geysers in Iceland, fjords in Norway or volcanoes in Sicily.

No pupil can go on every trip every year. Even if your child is in every sports team, is learning languages and would benefit from time as a language exchange student, *and* is studying geography, they do not need to go on a trip for each discipline each year. In fact, they don't need to go on an annual trip at all.

> *"Our son brought a letter home inviting him on a school ski trip to – you've guessed it – Whistler. A five day trip was going to cost around £1,600. Yes, he really, really wanted to go on the trip but, as we said, we've never been able to afford to learn to ski and, for that money, we could fund more than half of the cost of a family ski trip to Europe so that we could all learn. We said 'no'. We know that he might get invited on a school rugby trip in four years' time and that he might want to go on a geography field trip in three years' time. We want to be able to fund one of these, still manage a family holiday, and consider the fact that his younger sister might also want a school trip when it's her turn. For us, one trip is enough."*
>
> *Maddy*

PLAN AHEAD

The trick with school trips is to plan ahead. All schools tend to plan trips for pupils in certain age groups. So, it might be a language trip in Year 9, a geography trip in Year 10 and sports trips in each of the summers. Find out from other parents or from school information evenings what trips the school plans each year and use that information to plan ahead and budget for the trips you believe your child(ren) might benefit from the most.

Ask yourself:

□ What are your child's best subjects?

□ In which area will they get the most benefit from a trip?

□ What takes priority in your mind and that of your child: sports or curriculum-based trips?

11. Pocket money

Money makes the world go around and the sooner children understand what their money can buy, the better.

This chapter is not just about how much to give your children and when, it is also about how best to get your children to reach financial independence in a responsible way.

A look at the statistics, which are boxed out throughout this section, should cause some alarm. Quite frankly, they're meant to scare the pants off you. The statistics in this chapter are there to show where we, as adults, are going wrong and the monetary areas where today's children want more help and education. If we get it right, our children should be able to navigate their way through adulthood making fewer of the money mistakes that have dogged our generation.

Luckily, there has never been more information around than there is now to help us, as parents, bring our children up to be financially savvy and to get some tips for ourselves along the way.

Nearly all children are first introduced to the concept of pocket money in primary school. Pocket money is vital. It teaches children what things are worth; what they can buy immediately; what they need to save for; and how to apportion money between goodies for themselves, savings and gifts for friends and family. However, these skills do not come overnight.

> **The average weekly amount of pocket money is £6.32.**
>
> *(Source: Personal Finance Education Group at www.pfeg.org)*

Leading financial institutions such as Nationwide and Barclays have finally cottoned on to the fact that financially clued up kids means financially clued up adults – which means fewer indebtedness problems. As a result, they are helping schools to introduce age-appropriate financial education modules.

By 2011, financial education will be a compulsory element of the national curriculum in both primary and secondary schools in England and Wales, which is great news. So, from identifying the value of different coins age five to analysing budgets age 14, children will be schooled in how to manage money.

> **66% of Britons believe finance lessons would have helped them deal with today's financial challenges.**
>
> *(Source: www.pfeg.org)*

As with all subjects and education, not everything can be learned at school: homework – and parental support – plays a vital role. Just as children of smokers are more likely to end up as smokers themselves, so children of shopaholics are likely to copy those behaviours in adulthood. None of us want to lead our children to a life of financial problems, therefore our role as parents is to instil monetary behaviours that will help rather than hinder our children as they enter adulthood.

> **28% of parents have no savings and 20% of parents have less than £1,000 to fall back on.**
>
> *(Source: Abbey Savings)*

Getting started

PRE-SCHOOL

In today's consumer society, children are adept shoppers long before they are old enough to receive pocket money. They know what they want to buy from a very young age, but may not know what it costs or whether they have enough pocket money with which to buy it.

Pre-school (age three to five) is the age when children love playing with coins, even if it's just to feel them, all cold and shiny in their little palms. So, this is the time when parents can capitalise on that and introduce money into their play.

Playing shop

Boys and girls love playing shop. Toy manufacturers are wise to this and have produced a never ending stream of replica plastic shopping items for this purpose. The thing is they're not real; children know they're not real, so they're not as fun as playing with the real thing. Instead, save yourself a fortune and make your own shop.

- □ Collect, over time, a selection of different value coins.
- □ Convert a shoe box into a home-made till using cardboard compartments (being a wine lover, I find the cardboard wine bottle carriers are great for this sort of thing!).
- □ Instead of buying replica items to fill the 'shop', recycle real packaging for the job.
- o Biscuit and cereal boxes are fine as they are.
- o Milk and juice cartons can be washed out.
- o The cardboard sleeves on meat packaging can be used instead of the real thing.
- □ A greengrocer's shop can be made any time from the contents of your fridge. What's more, there are no storage issues, as everything goes back into the kitchen cupboards afterwards.

❝❝ My children are learning slowly how far their money will go. That's been helped a great deal by websites like Club Penguin. If they want to subscribe to that, I deduct the cost of it from their pocket money. So, instead of receiving £2 a week they will only get £1. This has really helped them to see that online purchases are real and it helps them to choose where and how they want to spend their money. 🗏🗏

Jan, mum to Ben and Charlie

The value of loose change

Giving your child the loose change from the bottom of your purse is a great way to start the pocket money ball rolling. This doesn't have to be done on a regular basis. In fact, at this stage, it is probably much better if it is done sporadically. Over the course of a week your child might not be given more than 20p in 1p and 2p coins. However, once a month, that could be spent at the corner shop. It would buy a decent bag of sweets or even cover half the cost of a magazine. So, without getting into a formal pocket money arrangement, your child would start to understand, slowly and surely, what money could buy.

STARTING SCHOOL

Starting school is where lessons in managing money really begin. In the infant years (age five to seven), children are ready to learn about:

- ◻ Different coins and notes that we use
- ◻ How to count money
- ◻ Working out what change we are owed
- ◻ What money can buy and how far it stretches
- ◻ Money used overseas – eg counting and spending in euros or dollars etc
- ◻ Keeping money safe

Over time, regular forays into shops with money will also begin to teach children of this age group that it is not possible to buy everything that we want; that sometimes things have to be saved for and that sometimes they will make bad spending decisions.

How much to give and how to give it

❝ Both boys like to buy a magazine each week, which cost £1.90 each, so they both get £2 a week if they've been good. ❞

Jan, mum to Ben and Charlie

❝ Lauren and Isabella are now at the age where they can earn money for little tasks, such as helping me mind baby Mia, or tidying away the washing. Tasks like that earn 20p a time. ❞

Lisa, mum to Lauren, Isabella and Mia

❝ Both boys have a maximum amount they can earn each week. Carter is older so he can earn £1.50 a week. Charlie can earn £1.25. It means if they've been really naughty, I can deduct 10p or 20p that day but if they've been good they get the full amount. It matters because they both know exactly what they want to spend the money on. ❞

Lisa, mum to Carter and Charlie

Money is an emotive subject among children and adults alike. There is always going to be one child in the class that has every toy going and earns more pocket money than any of their classmates. While your child might moan 'not fair' at you for falling short in the pocket money stakes, you are providing a better life lesson. Having a limited amount of pocket money means your child will have to make choices about what to spend their money on and what to save up for from an early age, and therefore stand a better chance of getting into a good savings habit.

HOW MUCH

Leading Child Trust Fund provider, The Children's Mutual, has collated average pocket money statistics for its *Pocket Money Guide*. They provide a useful benchmark for parents trying to work out just what an appropriate level of pocket money might be.

Age	Average weekly pocket money
5	£1.48
6	£1.64
7	£2.04
8	£1.98
9	£2.60
10	£2.70
11	£2.44
12	£3.32
13	£3.43
14	£4.27
15	£5.66

(Source: The Children's Mutual Pocket Money Guide)

National averages can give us an idea of whether our children will be broadly in line with their peers in pocket money stakes. Clearly they should only be used as a rough guide. Otherwise, if parents were to take these averages literally, our children would be complaining bitterly at age eight, and again at age 11 when they have had a drop in their weekly pocket money in real terms. Personally, I think both ages are a little too young for them to be having such harsh credit crunch lessons.

HOW TO GIVE IT

In its *Pocket Money Guide*, The Children's Mutual says that making children earn their pocket money might seem like a good idea from a grown up's perspective. However, this approach does not necessarily yield the spend/ save results parents are hoping to instil.

> **Children who earned pocket money were less likely to save it. They saw it as earned cash that they could spend immediately.**
>
> *(Source: The Children's Mutual Pocket Money Guide)*

As parents, this could provide a stumbling block. After all, most of us want to instil in our children the twin virtues of working to earn money and saving a portion of that money.

There are two ways this can be handled:

□ Divide pocket money into two elements: one half that is apportioned as of right; the other half that is earned.

◻ Have a set weekly pocket money amount but reserve the right to 'top it up', perhaps if your child has done something special. (Perhaps your top-ups can also help your child save up for something special.)

❝❝ The tooth fairy has an exorbitant pricing system these days. Where we live (in Manchester) the going rate seems to be £2 for a first tooth if it's REALLY shiny and £1 per tooth thereafter. I'm sure this depends on postcode but it's a lot more than when I lost my milk teeth. ❞❞

Caroline, mum to Sally and Sam

EARNING MONEY

"My children can earn pocket money when they help me to clean and vacuum out the car. They get paid a premium when it is particularly muddy! The point is, this is an 'extra' chore. It is not tidying their room, doing their homework or indeed anything else that we spend years training our children to realise forms part of their day-to-day responsibility."

Maddy

For children, it is important to know what their pocket money is for. That means it is also important to make it clear what you do not expect them to buy with it, as well as what you do. It is also worthwhile drawing up a list of chores you expect your children to do anyway, and those for which they can earn a few pennies. Here are some suggestions.

What parents buy	Expected chores	Extra 'earning' chores
• Clothes	• Homework	• Cleaning the car
• Books	• Making own bed	• Vacuuming
• Things for school	• Putting dirty clothes in the laundry basket	• Gardening
• Money for trips or school activities	• Putting clean clothes away	• Helping clean bedroom (wash windows, polish etc)
• Equipment for hobbies	• Keeping room tidy	• Watering plants
• Outings with friends	• Feeding/caring for their pet	• Washing up
	• Their designated house 'tasks', such as setting/clearing the table	• Helping to decorate
		• Helping with spring cleaning

Junior school

By the time children reach junior school (age eight to 11), they have a much clearer idea of what they need to do to earn their money, how far it will go (never far enough), and how to balance the conflicting demands of buying the comic they want now against saving for a bigger item later on.

By junior school age, children are also better able to handle a savings account. Many banks and building societies offer the parents of children the opportunity to convert a nominee savings account into one in the child's own name from the age of seven. (A nominee account is one a parent holds on behalf of their child.) Not all children will be ready at the age this facility is offered, so parents still have the choice to maintain a nominee account. Indeed, bank accounts for children should only be opened when those children are ready and willing to learn about saving.

> *"When my son turned seven I was sent a letter inviting me to change the nominee savings account I held on his behalf into a savings account in his name. I declined, deciding he was not ready to handle that responsibility. Eighteen months later I believe he is ready."*
>
> *Maddy*

In terms of the school curriculum, this ability to consider wider aspects of money means children are able to get to grips with more advanced financial concepts. By the time they leave junior school, most children should have learned about:

- Saving
- Different ways of saving
- Planning ahead with money
- Balancing needs and wants: balancing present and future buying decisions
- Value for money: good buys/bad buys
- Bank accounts
- Bank statements and how they work
- Making a simple budget and keeping records over time
- Forms of money other than cash: credit cards, debit cards, cheques, gift tokens
- How they work in broad terms

- ◻ How we earn money by working: how different jobs pay different levels of income
- ◻ The benefits system as a fall-back mechanism for those without work
- ◻ Pensions for those who have retired

The ethics of money

At junior school age, children become hugely aware of their immediate and wider environment. They start to get to grips with politics, with charity and why it matters. They also become aware that people have different standards of living. They know some of their friends have more money than others and they will become aware of where they fit in to this arbitrary pecking order.

This awareness can be broadened out. If you holiday abroad you can help your child to understand their relative spending power overseas. They can see just how many ice creams they can buy on holiday compared to at home. If your child takes an interest in the news, there are plenty of examples of stories that you can use to help them understand that being in financial control is a skill for life.

If your child has grandparents who have retired, you can explain how they can afford to live when they no longer work. Children want to understand how the mechanics of the adult world work and the sooner they get the broad concepts sorted in their heads, the longer they have to build their understanding up from that.

SAVING AND SPENDING

By the time your child reaches junior school years, they will have a pretty good idea of what things cost. No doubt they will have got wise to the concept of asking for a rise, or in volunteering for extra jobs around the time a new Nintendo DS game is being released! These are great skills to acquire and should be applauded. They can also be harnessed to help tweak that financial understanding a little further.

The pocket money increase

Many parents consider birthdays a sensible time to introduce a pay rise.

Other parents wait for their children to raise the issue, arguing that if they don't ask for more money, they don't need any more.

If your child does ask for an increase, perhaps you could consider getting them to argue their case? Get them to present their argument to you. They could show you what they spend their money on; what they consider to be a valued purchase; why they need more and what they would use it for. If they are the type of child who blows the entire pocket money stash the day they receive it, why not suggest that they try and save an element of their pocket money each week to put towards something other than their usual purchases?

You could have a deal with them so that if they save a little each week for a couple of months and manage to put it towards a longed-for item, you could give them a rise on the grounds that they have demonstrated they are ready for it. If, on the other hand, you have a child who already plans their spending and is sensible with it, then why not give a pay rise? Your child is clearly capable of handling it.

Wants vs needs

At this stage, everything for your child is a 'need'. Getting a child to understand the difference between something they 'want' and something they 'need' is very difficult. It is made more difficult by the fact that, as parents, you probably purchase all the things they need anyway.

Just because you buy all the necessary items, doesn't mean your child is incapable of understanding the difference. Indeed, it is vital that he or she learns the difference.

For adults, the sums are more difficult but the basic premise is simple: necessary bills such as the mortgage, insurances and utility bills must be paid first; after that comes food for the table and only when those essentials are taken care of can adults work out what they have left to spend on fun stuff. Showing your child how you work this out might help them to work out their own financial priorities. Everything might be a 'want' at this stage rather than a 'need' but your child will still have priorities.

TOP TIP: FUNDING LOST ITEMS

One of my children is particularly absent minded and quite clumsy. I got fed up with the amount of 'stuff' that would simply be lost at school. (Pens, goggles, football socks, shin pads etc.) In the end, we made a pact to teach him responsibility. I would buy everything he needed the first time. If he lost it, he would have to either buy the replacement from his pocket money if it was cheap, or pay a contribution towards the replacement if it was expensive. Having coughed up for a pair of goggles and a fountain pen, he has become far more aware of his possessions!

Good buys vs bad buys

This is an emotive subject, not least because most things children buy with their pocket money are bad buys when viewed through the jaded eyes of a parent. However, children are just learning to become consumers, so parents should expect there to be some mistakes along the way.

TEST CASE – THE SCHOOL FAIR

A good time to view whether your children make good or bad spending decisions is following a big event such as the school fair. School fairs are great because they give children the opportunity to let rip with their pocket money in a relatively safe environment. Some will blow their entire stash on the rides; others will gorge themselves on candy floss and fizzy drinks until they're sick. Others will spend ages choosing all manner of plastic tat (usually their own toys that you've 'recycled') from the white elephant stall.

Don't interfere with their spending decisions. Let them spend their money how they like. The following day, chat to them about what they spent their money on. Get your children to tell you what their best and worst buys were and why. Then you can chat about how they can avoid making some of those bad buys in the future.

We learn by making mistakes. When it comes to learning about money, we need to encourage our children to learn those lessons while they're still young. Giving them an environment in which they can make financial mistakes safely is important. What's more important, however, is the work you, as parents, do after the event in explaining how they could apportion their money better next time.

BUDGETING

Children of infant school age are able to put money aside for big things (sometimes). Junior age children can do this more consistently and are better able to articulate what they are doing and why. It's time to capitalise on that financial maturity.

BASIC FINANCIAL PLANNING (AGE SEVEN AND EIGHT)

Let's say your child gets £1.50 a week and likes to buy a magazine and sweets with that. The magazine costs £1.99; the sweets are 50p. Your child realises they don't get enough for the magazine, shrugs their shoulders and buys sweets every week. That's not the best outcome for anyone (other than your dentist).

Why not show them that, if they buy a 50p bag of sweets one week, they will have enough for the magazine the following week. They can have both, just not at the same time. In fact, show them that if they alternate – one week sweets, the following week magazines – they will not only have both items they want, they will also be saving money for other things that occur to them to buy later on (at a rate of 50p a fortnight).

Once your child is comfortable with basic planning, then it's time to throw more complex scenarios into the mix.

Most children get money at birthdays or Christmases from at least one relative. This can be incorporated into the basic financial plan alongside regular pocket money. If you've done your homework, your children should, by now, know that they should be putting something aside each time they get their money. It's time to apportion that more specifically.

Get your child to write four headings on top of four columns on a piece of paper:

Spend	Save (short-term)	Save (long-term)	Charity

Learning that we have a social conscience is an integral part of growing up, so establishing that within a pocket money routine is sensible.

Ask them to consider what portion of their money they should put into each. For example, if Granny gave them a tenner for their birthday, they probably want to go and find something worth £10 to spend it on. However, see what they decide. It might look something like this:

Spend £5	Save (short-term) £2	Save (long-term) £2.50	Charity 50p

Short-term savings might go towards bigger ticket items such as cinema trips or more expensive toys. Long-term savings would be putting money away for their future: perhaps to buy a car, to help with university spending money, or to help fund travel plans or a big school trip they know they will take in the future.

Now, throw in another issue. Raise the issue of family birthdays and Christmases and ask your child which pot they would use (bearing in mind the long-term savings pot is earmarked) to fund presents for friends and family?

In the end, your child's budgetary needs might look more like this:

Spend £3	Save (short-term) £2	Save (Long-term) £2.50	Presents £2	Charity 50p

Not all money your child receives should be split five ways. Sometimes, birthday money, for example, provides just the impetus to go and buy that big ticket item, such as new football boots or a computer game, so the spend and short-term save pots will merge. However, it is important for children to learn – and to keep track of – what money they receive, what they have spent that week, and what they have saved and where.

Pocket money dos and don'ts

Courtesy of The Children's Mutual *Pocket Money Guide*, here are some helpful dos and don'ts to get you started:

Do

- Give pocket money on the same day each week
- Let your child know what the pocket money is for
- Expect your child to make spending mistakes – sympathise rather than criticise when this happens

□ Give praise when your child manages their money well
□ Talk about how you manage your family finances, including any mistakes you make
□ Show your child how to keep pocket money records

Don't

□ Link pocket money with school performance
□ Give advances or loans
□ Expect your child to earn all their pocket money
□ Worry if your child makes unwise purchases from time to time
□ Worry if your child spends their money on things you consider of little value; they matter to the child
□ Expect your child to manage their money well immediately

For more information, or to download the *Pocket Money Guide*, go to **www. thechildrensmutual.co.uk/existing-customers/pocket-money.aspx**.

AFFORDING POCKET MONEY

It's all very well establishing what levels of pocket money average children receive, but this is still something parents have to try and fund. Different parents have different ways of tackling this issue.

❝ I always gave the girls their pocket money out of the child benefit. The minute I received that money, I put their pocket money to one side so I wouldn't spend it on anything else. ❞

Terri, mum to Rachel and Madeline

❝ I don't budget specifically for Ben and Charlie's pocket money. It comes out of my weekly spending money. ❞

Jan, mum to Ben and Charlie

❝ When the children were smaller I tried to give them their pocket money in different denominations of coins each week, to help them learn their money. So one week they had a whole pile of 5p coins and another week they'd have just two coins on the table. It taught them a lot about different values of coins and how they worked. It also meant I had to plan a lot and siphon off my loose change during the week so that I could give them a variety of coins on pocket money day. 🙸

Fiona, mum to Hollie and Fraser

Teenagers

If, by the time your child leaves primary school, he or she can plan their money, budget and divide what they receive into appropriate pots, you are well on your way to teaching them about financial responsibility as an adult.

Teenagers become financially aware very quickly and, the older your children get, the bigger the financial mistakes that they can make.

- 90% of teenagers say they worry about money on a daily basis
- 10 years is the average age at which children begin to purchase items online
- 51% of teenagers said they would like to learn how to control their spending

(Source: Personal Finance Education Group at www.pfeg.org)

Teenagers are being marketed to financially all the time. They have iPods and download tracks (for a fee, of course). They have mobile phones so they have financial contracts. They shop at Top Shop, where the Top Shop store card is touted by the store as 'the most fashionable way to pay'. In other words, they are getting financial messages all the time from big business. However, they may not have been taught to look behind the headlines of these messages to understand whether they are getting a good deal.

These years are critical. Teenagers have to learn to live within their means. That will mean learning to say 'no' when all they want to say is 'yes', and learning that money doesn't grow on trees.

Once they have learned those lessons, they need to learn how to make financial decisions. But first things first. This chapter is about pocket money and therefore it is about how parents can help their children learn good financial habits by increasing their financial freedom, in order that they may learn about financial responsibility.

ALLOWANCES

Opting to give your teenager an allowance is a sensible way to introduce wider financial responsibilities. However, as the parent, it is up to you to make it clear what that money is to be used for.

What you buy	What the allowance buys
• Transport to school	• Mobile phone credits
• Equipment for school and hobbies	• Music
• Food at home	• Going out
• School lunch or packed lunch	• Snacks
• Family meals out	• Meals out as entertainment with friends
• Ad-hoc academic expenses	• Presents for friends and family
• Wardrobe staples	

You still pick up the tab for the essential items in life, so if your teenager blows all their money on their mobile phone on the first day, you cover life's essentials until they're back on track.

There are some important lessons teenagers need to learn as part of their transition to adulthood and financial independence.

- □ Adults are paid monthly, not weekly (and months last longer than four weeks).
- □ A bank statement does NOT tell you how much money you have to spend.
- □ Living within your means gets harder, not easier, as you get older so get into the habit now.
- □ All financial deals are either a good deal or a bad deal. Learn to tell the difference between the two.

HOW OFTEN?

All the while your child is in primary school, giving pocket money on the same day each week is a great idea. Children can visualise taking their pocket money to a shop at the weekend and, if they blow the lot, they only have to wait another week before they can try again – and hopefully make a wiser decision.

In the real world, money doesn't work like that, so one of the greatest disservices you can do is to continue giving your child money every week. Adults are usually paid monthly and a key lesson your child needs to learn is that there are more than four calendar weeks in every month. You may scoff but I know adults who still assess how much they have to spend each week by dividing their pay packet into four. Then they wonder why they go overdrawn at the end of the month. Your teenagers will have to learn this lesson fast if they want to go out every weekend in a five-weekend month!

Once your child has put some money aside for savings, get them to look at the diary or calendar and see how many going out days they have to fund that month and how many weeks of phone credits they need to buy. It's a valuable lesson they simply cannot learn early enough.

HOW MUCH?

Child Benefit is paid to parents of all children in the UK until their child reaches age 16 or, if they are over 16, it will still be paid if they remain in education or training that still qualifies. It is set at a level of £20.30 week for the first child and £13.40 a week for second and subsequent children.

This is a level that has been designed to help parents raise their children. Obviously not everyone can afford to just hand over this money directly to teenagers who might blow the lot on iTunes downloads and unsuitable piercings. However, for those who can, and for those who have more than one child, it might be appropriate to split the difference between the allowances and use this as a guide to how much to hand over.

To put this into perspective, between two children that would mean an allowance each of £70 a month. If each child were compelled to save at least £20 of this for long-term savings, that leaves them £50 a month to spend (or £11.50 a week).

To put it another way, £70 a month sounds like a lot of money – and it will do to your teenager.

However, getting them to realise that £70 a month only equates to £11.50 a week, and that only means having around £5 a week to spend (having allocated money for weekly phone costs, short-term savings and presents) is a valuable lesson indeed.

It leaves enough money to either:
- □ Visit Starbucks twice a week with friends
- □ Pay for six iTunes downloads
- □ Buy one item of clothing from Top Shop once a month

SUPPLEMENTING THEIR INCOME

In today's consumer society, a fiver a week won't be enough to satisfy most teenagers. So, perhaps it is time to introduce the concept of supplementing that income. At 16, children are old enough to work on a casual basis in shops. Saturday jobs are a great way of earning more money and of understanding how much work produces how much money in the real world.

Supermarkets, high street shops, newsagents, theatres, cinemas, restaurants and hotels are all busy at weekends and therefore are great places for your child to go looking for paid employment. Some children relish the chance to earn money of their own; others cannot be bothered by it all. As parents, it is tempting to do what we do best: wave a magic wand and sort it all out for our child.

However, no matter how frustrated you are:
- □ Don't go and get a job for your child
- □ Don't bully them into work
- □ Don't give them a bigger allowance if they cannot live within their means and they're reluctant to work

Your teenager will rapidly realise that, without earning extra money, they simply don't have enough to buy the things they want and to socialise with their friends in the way they would like. To get round this they can either earn the difference or come begging to the bank of mum and dad to fund the difference.

THE CASE FOR A SATURDAY JOB

The national minimum wage for all workers under the age of 18 is currently £3.57 an hour. Your child, working an eight hour day once a week on a Saturday, could earn another £28 a week (or around £120 a month). Some jobs might also give your child the opportunity to increase their hours during the school holidays and earn a bit more to put aside ready for university or a summer holiday with friends. There's also the possibility that they will be offered more than the minimum wage. That's more like it!

Dealing with relatives

If you ask any parents whether they want a loving extended family for their children or not, most would say, 'Yes please' without hesitation. However, loving families bring their own issues to the table, not least the issue of over-indulgence.

Picture the scene: your teenage daughter has decided she wants to get her hair highlighted for her 15th birthday. You have talked it through with her and have agreed that, provided she saves up half the cost herself, you'll match that amount to help her achieve her goal. Granny hears of this plan and thinks it's a shame she has to wait so long and buys her the highlights as 'a little gift'.

It might be highlights; it might be money to go on holiday; a new games console or even a new iPod to replace the one she left on the bus. It doesn't matter what she is saving up for: it is important that she has to save up. The more children are made to save for things they really want, the more they value them when they get them and the more they appreciate how long it takes to purchase big ticket items.

Given that grannies are invariably pensioners, this issue shouldn't happen too frequently but it will happen and it will exasperate you precisely because it thwarts your attempts to teach a life lesson.

If Granny has already interfered and your daughter's hair sports yellow and orange fluorescent highlights, there's little you can do. However, if the money has been gifted but the hair appointment has not yet been made, there's still time to negotiate.

Those highlights won't be the only thing your daughter wants. Yet they are the thing she has chosen to save for, so she should continue to save for them. Have a word with Granny and see if she will agree to contribute to something else.

When dealing with relatives and money, there are some dos and don'ts to consider.

Don't

□ Lose your temper. Relatives are only trying to help.

□ Thwart your child's relationships with their extended family in order to retain control. At times when adolescence gets really ugly, you'll need the reassurance that your child feels able to talk to someone in the family.

□ Renege on your side of the savings bargain. Stick to it but explain that, next time, if your child gets financial help elsewhere it will be used instead of your financial contribution.

Do

□ Try to be tactful. Your daughter is their granddaughter/niece/ nephew too.

□ Remember that you were a teenager once.

□ Remember this is not a battle to retain control of your child; it is part of your child's financial education. There will be other ways to learn the same life lesson.

□ Speak to the relevant family member about this OUT OF EARSHOT of your child. Explain what you were trying to achieve by making them wait and making them save. You'll probably find the relative is on your side once they know the whole story.

Teenagers and debt

50% of teenagers have been in debt by the time they're 17

23% of teenagers tend to think of overdrafts as easy ways to spend more than they earn

(Source: Personal Finance Education Group at www.pfeg.org)

Teenagers still in full-time school education and living at home have no reason to get into debt. If they are then you – as a parent – have not done your job properly in explaining how to budget, how to save and how to make buying decisions.

The buying mantra:

- Do I need it?
- Can I afford it?
- Is it good value?

Do I need it?

This goes back to the lessons our children learned with their pocket money in primary school. Identifying the difference between 'wants' and 'needs' continues through into adulthood, yet it is this question, above all others, that leads people into financial difficulty.

If your teenager has trouble sticking to a budget, there's only one system to follow:

1. Go through their purchases with them.
2. Identify what they spent their money on.
3. Assess each purchase one by one. Ask them if they needed to buy that item. Ask them why they bought it. Ask them what they might have chosen to do with their money instead. Ask them which decision they would make, on balance, if they could do so again.

Can I afford it?

This is a simple but dangerous issue. This is where we need to practise what we preach in order to teach our children how to spend responsibly.

So, ask yourself whether you have ever purchased anything with a credit card because you had no other means of buying that item. Then consider how many of those purchases were necessary. (Items such as car tyres or food for the family might be considered essential; clothes, meals out or holidays are not essential, no matter how much you might want one.) If you have used credit to buy something you 'want' rather than 'need', then perhaps you and your teenager should draw up a spending pact together. Watch each other's spending (you'll hate it even more than your child!). It is a brutal but effective way of changing spending patterns.

Is it good value?

Let's consider for a second that your child is financially responsible and living within their means. Does that mean they are making good buying decisions? Not necessarily. If they are an impulse shopper then the answer is most definitely not. Something is good value if you have acquired it for the best possible price in a way that is most convenient to you. That means doing some research before you buy anything. So, show your savvy, switched on child how to research prices on comparison websites while internet shopping and while shopping in the high street and you'll have taught them a life lesson.

Do as I do, not as I say

Teenagers may be surly and rebellious but they still have minds like sponges that absorb a great deal more than we tell them. They absorb behaviours and ways of living subconsciously, so, don't let your lack of savings or your spending binges lead to financial problems for your children in adulthood.

- □ If you save, your children are more likely to save.
- □ If they see you planning your finances on a regular basis, they are more likely to plan their own finances.
- □ If you explain how you pay for Christmas or afford a family holiday, they will see that handling money is a life skill.
- □ If you cannot earn more you must spend less.

12. The future and financial independence

One day our children will fly the nest. One day they may have children of their own and will be responsible for raising another generation to adulthood. For the moment, we, as parents, face some daunting final hurdles: teaching our children to stand on their own two feet; to pay for themselves without getting into debt; to hold down a job, keep a roof over their heads and pay the bills.

This is not as easy as it sounds – and it is becoming harder.

University is becoming more expensive to fund and average house prices are steadily rising at the same time as lenders require larger and larger deposits to secure decent loan rates. So many adults, still repaying debt from their student years, are trying to save at the same time for a deposit. If not, they have to save for rental deposits knowing it's virtually impossible to get that money back again.

The alternative, of course, is to move back in with mum and dad (provided they haven't rented out their child's old bedroom to give them something to live on in retirement!).

In a nutshell, your child has to be financially savvy very, very quickly or their manageable debt mountain will turn into an unmanageable debt burden in moments.

STUDENT DEBT – THE FACTS

- **58% of postgraduates are still paying off debt in their mid-thirties.**
- **The standard student loan while at university is £12,000.**

(Source: Student Gems)

- **Students who started their studies in autumn 2009 can expect to graduate with debts of £23,500.**

(Source: the Push student debt survey)

- **Average graduate debt in 2004 was £12,069, a rise of 10% on the previous year. Students who attended university in the South West had the highest average debt at £14,802, compared to students in the Midlands, who had the lowest average debt at £11,484.**

(Source: Barclays' 10th annual student debt survey, published May 2004)

These numbers are scary. No wonder more students are looking to study near home, or are boomeranging back to the parental home once they've graduated. Many simply cannot afford to do anything else.

So, while your child is still living at home and studying at school, they are not only financially care-free but also a captive audience. It's time to teach some financial life lessons.

Types of student debt

Once at university, there will be a myriad of finance options available to your child. There will be student loans and overdrafts. There may even be credit cards and your child will also be eligible to apply for store cards, cable TV contracts, monthly mobile phone tariffs, and even car finance.

As an adult, think about how you regard these forms of finance and think how comfortable you would be for your child to opt for some of these.

> *"Personally, I'd hate my 18-year-old to land at university, go*
> *shopping in fresher's week and sign up for a store card."*
>
> *Maddy*

As a parent, it's not enough to say that store cards are devil spawn and should never, ever, on pain of death, be taken out. I could tell my children that their exorbitant rates of interest will always outweigh any 10% discount the card might give shoppers on an introductory deal, but since when has any teenager listened to their parents' advice away from home?

Unless children understand the reasons why some financial decisions are bad, they'll make financial mistakes. And, if they do make financial mistakes and end up in a spiral of uncontrollable debt, who will they turn to for help? That's right: your paltry life savings are at stake if you get this wrong!

Nobody has a snappier way with money advice than Money Saving Expert Martin Lewis, so I'm going to refer liberally to his mantras. These are all found in his Teen Cash Guide which you can download from his website: **www.moneysavingexpert.com/teencash**.

❝ Debt isn't bad; bad debt is bad. ❞

Martin Lewis, Money Saving Expert

STUDENT LOANS

Good debt. Interest is pegged at the rate of inflation, nothing more, and payments are deferred until graduates earn above a certain threshold (currently set at £15,000). Repayments were set at 9% of gross income and the repayment threshold is due to be reviewed in 2010. However, in a nutshell, this is the cheapest type of debt your child can take and is therefore a good deal.

OVERDRAFTS

Authorised = OK; unauthorised = seriously bad news. Overdrafts can be bad news when they are 'unauthorised'. In other words, if you borrow more than your pre-arranged borrowing limit, you will be charged a fortune. However, stick within that limit and overdrafts can be a cheap way of accessing money on an ad hoc basis.

Students need overdrafts. Unless your child has worked solidly for a year before attending university and has built up a sizeable savings pot, AND is very careful with money, they will use an overdraft. Many banks offer overdrafts of up to £3,000 to students. The catch is to see how quickly they cease to become interest-free once your chid has graduated! Some banks give students six months after graduation before they 'convert' their account into a normal bank account with normal levels or charges; other banks give students a little longer and call it a graduate account.

The bank that offers the best deal for students will probably not be the bank that offers the best deal for graduates. Teach your child that financial loyalty rarely pays. Tell them to develop a cynical streak – and fast – if they want to avoid the nightmare scenario of banks ramping up interest charges and effectively adding whole new layers to their debt.

CREDIT CARDS

Bad debt. Credit cards are a dangerous option for students because of the temptation to use them when there is no visible means of repaying that debt. However, many companies market to students to get them to be brand loyal from the word go (and to maximise their earnings over that student's adult life).

Your child needs to know how quickly a small credit card debt can turn into an unmanageable debt mountain and the quickest way to do that is to give them a lesson in compound interest.

COMPOUND INTEREST

Scenario One

Say your child runs up a credit card debt of £1,000 in freshers' week, on a card with an APR of £20%.

- □ After a year they will owe £1,200
- □ After two years they will owe £1,440
- □ After three years they will owe £1,728
- □ Now, they've graduated in a bit of a recession and haven't found a job for a year, so by the end of year four they will owe £2,074

In other words, their debt has more than doubled due to the dubious charms of compound interest (or, to put it more simply, interest that gets charged on the interest as well as on the original debt).

However, it's not enough to know that compound interest hurts. Your child needs to understand how to turn this knowledge into the ability to choose between financial products.

Take an example Money Saving Expert Martin Lewis put to a class of teenagers for his *Teen Cash Guide*.

THE TEEN CASH CLASS'S QUIZ

Question: Should you take a lower rate for longer; or a higher rate for shorter?

Imagine you have a mortgage, and because the lender is secure in the knowledge it can take the house back if you can't repay, it gives you a cheap rate of, say, 6%. Now you need an additional loan for a car and the best interest rate you can find is 12%. Suddenly, your mortgage lender says, 'Hey, why not borrow that extra £10,000 on top of your mortgage? After all, at 6%, it's half-price...'

Martin asked his Teen Cash Class which they thought was better. Understandably, they all went for the cheaper rate. This would be good... except... a typical loan will be paid back over five years, while most mortgages last for 25 years.

Here's the real answer:
- A £10,000 loan at 12% over five years costs £3,300 in interest
- £10,000 added to a mortgage at 6% over 25 years costs £9,200 in interest

As you can see, the higher interest rate loan is much cheaper. Though it does also mean because you need to pay it more quickly you need to repay more a month.

(Source: Money Saving Expert Martin Lewis)

So it's not enough for your child to know how much they intend to borrow: they need to know how long it's for. This is where it pays to be realistic.

Most of us are optimistic about the future. Young adults are no exception.

They believe (quite rightly) that going to university will enable them to get a well paid job, making the debt burden they carry a worthwhile sacrifice. However, what they underestimate is the length of time it takes for those reasonable earnings to kick in.

You can see from Martin's example that the length of a loan is just as important as the rate of the loan. So, when your child graduates, sit down together; look at the financial options (for things other than the official student loan); and work out together what is the cheapest/most affordable strategy for debt repayment.

REPAYMENT OPTIONS

You and your graduate offspring may also need to think flexibly when it comes to tackling student debt. Graduates are still in their career infancy and may need to chop and change jobs or indeed retrain because a stable career path becomes clear. If this happens, their earnings might change dramatically. On each occasion this happens, it is important that your graduate sits down and re-works the sums. They may or may not want help with this (not all graduates are honest with their parents about the level of debt they have run up) but if they will let you help, two heads are better than one.

> - **Over half (51%) of students underestimated how long it would take them to repay debts by more than three years.**
> - **7% underestimated the duration by more than 10 years.**
> - **Students expected, on average, to have repaid their debts by the age of 28, although research indicated that the true figure is likely to be 31.**
>
> *(Source: the Debt Perception Report)*

How you can help

As a parent, not only can you help your child financially during their university years, you can also help by preparing them for adulthood so that they are able to take the tough financial decisions in an appropriate way. If you fund your child through university and do not teach the fundamentals of making appropriate financial choices, you simply defer the mistakes he or she will make.

It's time to let your kids understand how you run a house, how you make your financial decisions and how often you review your family's financial position.

There are two lessons your child needs to learn from you:

1. How to monitor spending and work out how much you really have to spend
2. How you can increase that

LESSON 1: MONITORING SPENDING

Bank statements: what you see ain't what you get

How often do you look at the state of your bank account? If you bank online, the answer is probably at least once a week. Throughout the teenage years, it is time to introduce your child to the concept that what they see is not what they get.

Say it's the beginning of the month and you've just been paid. Let's assume you're on a decent salary and your account is sitting pretty with £3,000 in it. Being a sensible and responsible adult, you have arranged for many of your direct debits and standing orders to leave your account at the beginning of the month to ensure greater control over your spending.

Week One

Item	Amount	Balance
		3,000
Mortgage	1,500	1,500
Council tax	200	1,300
Contents/building insurance	50	1,250
Car insurance	60	1,190
Life insurance	50	1,140
Income protection	150	990
Savings – ISA	150	840
Savings – holiday	200	640
Savings – Christmas	50	590
Kids/hobbies	50	540
Food	80	460
Remainder		460

The biggest trap people fall into is to assume that the money they have sitting in their bank account is money available to spend.

Ask your child, 'How much do you have to spend?' Their answer might be £460 but that's not right, and here's why:

Week Two

Item	Amount	Balance
		460
Water rates Food	51 80	409 329
Remainder		329

Now your child might be getting the idea that sometimes, when you change utility companies, they start direct debits on different days in the month, so not all bills are paid in the first week. Food is an ongoing cost and so you will be paying out a substantial sum on a weekly basis. Now you can start to talk to your child about how to assess what you really have to spend.

Here are the assumptions your child needs to make in order to assess how much spending money you have:

□ It is a five-week month
□ Your electricity and gas bill has not yet left your account (£95)
□ You will be paid Child Benefit of £134.80 (based on two children and paid four-weekly)

The answer is:

In		Out		Balance
				329
Child benefit	134.80	Fuel Food	95 240	
				128.80

You can show your child that, once you have accounted for everything and squirrelled the appropriate amounts away into the appropriate pots so you can pay for holidays/Christmas/football subs and school trips, you have a grand total of £128.80 to spend FOR THE ENTIRE MONTH. That works out at around £25 a week, so don't spend it all at once.

This is a lesson your child needs to learn – and fast.

LESSON TWO: HOW TO INCREASE YOUR SPENDING MONEY

There are two options:

- □ Earn more
- □ Spend less on the boring stuff so you've got more left over for the fun stuff

The earlier your child understands this, the better.

At this point they (and you) might question why you 'waste' so much money on insurance and income protection. In the depths of our monthly financial juggling, it often seems like a valid question. For the full answer, read Chapter 4, which explains all the options about protecting yourself and your family: why this matters and what can happen if you don't. For the moment, assume these insurances are non-negotiable and they are also the best value.

So, where can you save money?

In Chapter 7, I detailed how you can go through your monthly expenditure forensically and cut bills. That process is not a one-off; it is an annual event. This means, during your child's teenage years, there will be five occasions when he can help you with this process. Think of it as essential life training.

Kids love the internet. They are web savvy. They also love a challenge.

The Challenge

Let your child loose on comparison websites – and show them the Money Saving Expert guides – and see if they can save you money on your household bills.

This is how you can see what your child has learned and see if they are able to discern good 'value' from 'good headlines'. If you've done your homework, they'll read the small print and get to grips with a product's complete picture. If not, this is the perfect time to teach them that the headline-grabbing rates you see at the start of a credit card offer, for example, aren't always what you get.

You could be surprised. They might be better at this bill-cutting business than you. Whatever the outcome, this is practical real-life economising that can only stand your child in good stead.

LESSON THREE: MANAGING ACCOUNTS

By this, I don't just mean making sure you don't go overdrawn at the end of the month. Look at the monthly expenditure example above: there are three different savings amounts scheduled to leave that account as well as a fourth, labelled 'kids' that might be instant access savings under another name. Why don't I just lump them all together and put them in one top-paying account?

The answer is simple and it goes back to how you teach your child to manage pocket money with four different labelled 'pots'. Let's find another example to illustrate this.

THE FAMILY HOLIDAY

Let's say that this year, I couldn't find a family holiday we all wanted to go on for less than £3,000. I thought, never mind, I've got plenty of savings elsewhere. Why don't I just take some money out of my ISA to make up the difference?

Ask your child, would that be a good idea or a bad idea?

On the face of it, that could be a good idea. I've not gone into debt to finance the holiday; it is money I have put aside and, let's say, over the last couple of years that pot has built up to £3,600. Surely I won't miss £600?

That depends. What I need to know before I answer that question is, what it the ISA money there for?

- Is it rainy day money (to fix a leaky roof, replace windows etc)?
- Is it saving up to replace the car in five years' time?

Is it the only savings I will have to live off in old age because I don't have a company pension?

Looking back at the bank account in my example, there is no other way of saving up contingency money so I'd say it was there to do one or more of these jobs. Therefore, it would be a bad idea to dip into this pot to pay for the holiday.

I should therefore just be thankful I can afford a holiday at all and widen the search until I get what I want at the right price. Alternatively, the family could forego their holiday this year and we could save up for a bigger, better holiday the year after.

The holiday is there as an example to illustrate how easy it is to merge pots of money together that should be allocated for very different purposes.

Bank accounts are free to open and free to run. What's more, there is no limit on the number of bank accounts an individual can operate. So, have a different account for each different purpose.

> *"I'm self employed, so my earnings are variable to say the least. However, I still have to pay for karate lessons once a term, new school shoes when the children's feet have grown, and football subs and coaching for my son's club. So, each time I'm paid I divert a proportion of my earnings to a separate bank account, which I only use for the children. In fact, I segregate money into different funds for all manner of other things too."*
>
> *Maddy*

I thought I'd taken things to ridiculous extremes until I got talking to a group of women. They all do the same.

I think it is no coincidence they all (me included) have worked, at one time or another, for a bank or building society.

TOP TIP: SEPARATE SAVINGS POTS FOR SEPARATE SAVINGS GOALS

Take a leaf out of children's savings techniques and open a different savings account for each savings pot: one for kids' hobbies, one for Christmas, one for holidays, one for a rainy day. Label them clearly and siphon money into each accordingly. Most women I know who have ever worked in banking do exactly that.

So, the lesson we teach our primary-age children with different savings 'pots' for different purposes should be a lesson we apply to our adult finances. Show your teenager that you have separate funds. Divide them according to:

- Holiday
- Christmas
- Children
- Rainy day (long-term) savings
- Clothes/birthdays/outings

Keep them separate and explain why you do this. Children follow the financial patterns of their parents. You remain the most influential role model and can use that to extraordinary effect.

LESSON FOUR: THE POWER OF LONG-TERM SAVINGS

The university debt burden can be lessened considerably if you have begun a savings habit that your children can continue.

Way, way back in Chapter 4, I looked at children's savings accounts and how much you would have stashed away for your child if you just sidelined £20 a month. That could be in a regular savings account, a Bonus Bond, a Child Trust Fund or some form of regular savings, feeding into the best long-term savings product on the market.

How you do it is up to you: the fact that you have done it at all will reduce your child's debt burden upon graduation by years.

Siphoning off £20 a month from the minute your child is born means you will have put aside £4,320 of your money by the time your child reaches adulthood. However, just as compound interest can have a negative effect on your money when it comes to debt, it can also have a truly remarkable effect on your money when it comes to saving – particularly long-term saving.

TOP TIP: SAVE LITTLE AND OFTEN

£20 a month will give your child a cash pot of around £5,921 by the time they reach age 18 and want to head off to university. In today's prices, that would cover a quarter of a student's anticipated debt upon graduation.

Working to bridge the earnings gap

> - Almost three quarters (73%) of university students worked in 2009 to help fund their studies.
> - That rose from 66% of students the previous year.
> - Nearly half of students (46%) have a part-time job during term time.
> - Students with part-time jobs worked an average of 13.5 hours a week.
> - Students feel the pinch more during the latter years of their degrees.
> - 81% of students in their final year said they had a job during the holidays to help fund their studies.
>
> *(Source: Halifax Student Panel research, which polled 60,000 students)*

Getting your child to realise that paid work will be a necessary part of student life is important. More important, however, is the realisation that your child can start saving much earlier.

Having read Chapter 11 – all about pocket money – and the first part of this chapter – about financial independence – you will appreciate that, as a caring, sharing, responsible parent, money knowledge means money control. No doubt, therefore, your child already knows about the £20 a month you put away for university education. However, that is not enough. It's time to ask yourself:

- □ Does my child know how far that money will go?
- □ Does my child know how to make up the shortfall?
- □ Can I help my child put a plan in place to do this?

HELPING TO BRIDGE THE GAP BEFORE UNIVERSITY BEGINS

In Chapter 11, we looked at how much your child could earn by getting a Saturday job from the age of 16 to help fund their lifestyle while still at home. My example showed that, based on the minimum wage for workers under the age of 18 being £3.57 an hour, your child could earn around £120 a month for a Saturday job.

Having already taught your child to compartmentalise money the minute they get it (remember those different pocket money pots?), you could ask how much of their earnings they plan to save over the two years before they head off to university.

    □ Saving £50 a month would give your child at least £1,200 before interest – more like £1,300 when interest has been applied (assuming savings rates of 5%).

    □ Saving £60 a month – or half those earnings – would give your child £1,440 before interest. An interest rate of 5% would increase that pot to nearly £1,550.

GAP YEARS

In the glorious days of the early 1990s as student loans were just being introduced, it was common for A-Level graduates to take a gap year and spend their time travelling around on an elongated holiday. Not any more. These days, more and more students are using gap years as an opportunity to earn as much money as possible before they embark on their chosen course.

Many students might be able to find gainful employment that pays more than the minimum wage. However, as shift work and bar work remain popular choices for gap year students, this example has been based on minimum wage calculations.

The minimum wage for 18-21 year olds is currently £4.83.

(Source: www.direct.gov.uk)

THE POWER OF THE GAP YEAR

WORKING FOR SIX MONTHS DURING A GAP YEAR

If your child gets a job working five days a week, they could earn just over £800 a month (based on an eight hour day). So after six months they will have earned around £5,000, which falls below the level at which basic rate tax is payable (currently £6,475).

Now, your child is over 18 you no longer receive Child Benefit. So, bye bye parental allowance. And, given that your child is earning more, no doubt they want to keep more of their earnings to spend each week. So, let's assume your child saves £600 a month and spends £200. That means, by working for just 6 months, your child can save £3,600 towards university costs.

Using the same calculations, your child could save £5,400 towards university if they worked for nine months. That would fund another quarter of their anticipated debt upon graduation.

HOW MUCH IS ENOUGH?

No-one can estimate how much it will cost to fund a degree just by looking at the average debt levels of recent graduates. Luckily, Halifax asked students what they spent in an average week during term time.

DURING THE UNIVERSITY TERM

- Country-wide, students spent a weekly average of £193.50
- The weekly spend for London-based students was £247.90

(Source: Halifax Student Panel research)

Taking the national average and extrapolating it across a 30-week university year, that would mean students spend £5,805 a year.

However, that's not the end of the story. Only students who live in university halls of residence pay accommodation just during term time (which is probably less than half the student population). The rest of the students have to pay accommodation from mid-September through to early July – eight weeks more than this calculation. Including accommodation and utility bills for a further eight weeks, therefore, increases the bill to £7,353.

So, the average cost for your child to attend university each year is £7,353.

In other words, your child's six months of gap year earnings PLUS their £1,500 of Saturday job money could almost fund their first year. Your £20 a month savings you have squirrelled away from birth could fund a similar proportion of their second or third years.

BALANCING WORK AND PLAY

Naturally, if your child has worked hard all through school, got good grades AND has secured a good job to help fund university, they might just want to let their hair down and party for a couple of months of that gap year.

So, why not suggest that they work for 10 months? Put £600 aside for seven months to fund further education (£4,200) and use the remaining three months' money (£1,800) to fund their travel. If this doesn't meet the cost of their grand plan, you could always consider making up the difference, particularly if they have worked hard and saved responsibly. After all, they're only young once!

How to handle the boomerangs

- 25% of men aged 25–29 live with their parents
- More than 10% of men in their early 30s still live with their mum and dad

(Source: Office for National Statistics)

There are various names for these (predominantly male) children who come back to the safety of the parental nest:

- ▫ Kippers – kids in parents' pockets
- ▫ Boomerang children – children returning to the family home after graduation

Whatever you want to call them, children are increasingly returning home after graduation, not least because of rising living costs, increased graduate unemployment and rising levels of student debt.

In many ways they are victims of the university success. The number of undergraduates has tripled since 1970 from 414,000 to 1.27 million a year. Now, it doesn't take a rocket scientist to work out that there are not suddenly 800,000 more highly paid, appropriate jobs for graduates now than there were in the 1970s, despite whatever economic growth may have occurred in the meantime.

In other words, your child may not get the job they want or need despite going to get a degree and shouldering a debt burden in the process.

IF THEY CAN'T GET A JOB

There is a fine line parents must walk between encouraging, motivating and nagging. Your child might be an adult and a graduate but they are still your child and will react accordingly. If they are genuinely trying to get employment, then don't nag. Encourage in other ways:

- ▫ See if they want you to try and use any contacts you have.
- ▫ Offer to revise their CV.

□ While they're living rent-free at home, encourage them to
do volunteer work or unpaid internships within their chosen
profession to gain experience.

If they have got a job, and an appropriate one at that, then it's time to
consider charging rent.

CHARGING YOUR CHILDREN

❝I charge David £200 a month rent. I do his washing and ironing
and that money includes utility bills, but I don't buy his food,
nor would he expect me to. Yes he's paying me less than the
market rate, but I'm happy to support him because I can see
he's working really hard and he's saving up ready to move out
and rent a flat with his mates. ❞

> Sian, mum to Jess and David

There is nothing wrong with charging your children rent. They have been
paying accommodation costs since they were 18 or 19 in various student
digs so they are perfectly used to the concept. Before you raise the issue
with your children though, think about:

□ What is the going rate for a room in your area?
□ Do you want to keep the fridge stocked or is that their
responsibility?
□ Will you be doing their washing and ironing? Should this be
included?
□ Will you pay the council tax and the phone bill or do you
expect them to contribute their share?
□ Are you a convenient slave or is there more to this
arrangement?

When you have decided what you believe is reasonable, raise the issue with
your child. Tell them you want to charge them rent and suggest they come
up with a level they consider is appropriate.

See if you can agree on a rate you both find acceptable

Once you have agreed an acceptable rate then you have to work out what
you believe that rate includes. From their perspective, they probably expect

it to include everything, from ironed boxer shorts to breakfast in bed! So, go through all the extras, such as cleaning, washing, food, phone bills, cable and decide, item by item, what you will.

Once it is agreed, write this down

It may seem ridiculous to have a written agreement with your own child but they are an adult and they would have a rental contract in any other situation, so treat this as such.

EXTRA PARENTAL RESPONSIBILITIES

Do you at this stage have any more parental responsibilities? You could argue that you have already raised your children. Saved for them, taught them financial independence (or not), and still they're at home paying sub-market rates and expecting star treatment so there's nothing more you can do.

You'd be wrong.

Consider at this point whether your child would still live with you if they could get the same standard of accommodation at the same price somewhere else. The answer in most cases would be a resounding 'no'.

In other words, your child is in a Catch-22 situation. They earn, but not enough to afford a place of their own; they work so they want a decent standard of accommodation. We've all been there ourselves so it's time to think creatively.

Charge them the market rate for rent and save half

One way to help them solve this issue is to charge them the going rate to rent their old room but to save half of this rent for their future deposit. If, for example, you charge £100 a week in rent and save £50, after two years you will have saved them more than £5,500 (assuming 5% interest). After five years, you will have saved them more than £15,000 (assuming no rent rises).

Children need financial help long after they have become adults. That doesn't necessarily mean that you, as parents, will be permanently funding them. It could mean you simply provide them with the wherewithal to stand on their own two feet with more certainty than they could manage just by muddling through on their own.

Final word

No one can ever know all there is to know about raising a family, and there are as many ways of raising children as there are families busy doing just that, day in, day out.

This book hasn't been written as a definitive guide and I hope it won't be treated as such. Hopefully it explains how much some of the main child-rearing options cost and perhaps how some aspects of financing a family might be tackled.

This book is never going to provide all answers to all parents – that would be an impossible task. Indeed, for every question I posed to parents up and down the country I got many different replies. In one memorable instance there was a group debate going on across facebook between women who'd never met, about everything from what constituted essential baby kit to the cost of the tooth fairy!

I just hope that, by laying bare some of the costs and options involved in common family decisions, this book can help you make up your own mind about how best to approach the issues to suit your family circumstances and your ambitions for your children.

I'm still learning and I'm sure my two children will be the first to say that I'm forever making mistakes. I've certainly learnt a lot while compiling the data for this book and I hope my kids reap the benefit of that wisdom (although I'm sure they'll argue otherwise).

So goodbye, good luck and happy parenting.

Maddy

Useful websites

Advice
Citizens Advice Bureau: www.citizensadvice.org.uk
Which?: www.which.co.uk

Parenting
Baby Kind: www.babykind.co.uk
Bounty: www.bounty.com
Mumsnet: www.mumsnet.com
NCT: www.nct.org.uk
Netmums: www.netmums.com

Comparison sites and money advice
The Children's Mutual Pocket Money Guides: www.thechildrensmutual.co.uk
Confused: www.confused.com
Go Compare: www.gocompare.com
Money Facts: www.moneyfacts.co.uk
Money Saving Expert: www.moneysavingexpert.com
Money Supermarket: www.moneysupermarket.co.uk

Government
Benefits: www.entitledto.co.uk
Child Trust Fund: www.childtrustfund.gov.uk
HMRC: www.hmrc.gov.uk
Direct Gov: www.direct.gov.uk

Shopping and sourcing
Freecycle: www.freecycle.org
Supermarket: www.mysupermarket.co.uk
Voucher codes: www.vouchercodes.co.uk

Index